Oxford Junior Rhyming Dictionary

OXFORD
UNIVERSITY PRESS

Great Clarendon Street, Oxford OX2 6DP

Oxford University Press is a department of the University of Oxford.
It furthers the University's objective of excellence in research, scholarship,
and education by publishing worldwide in

Oxford   New York

Auckland Cape Town Dar es Salaam Hong Kong Karachi
Kuala Lumpur Madrid Melbourne Mexico City Nairobi
New Delhi Shanghai Taipei Toronto

With offices in

Argentina Austria Brazil Chile Czech Republic France Greece
Guatemala Hungary Italy Japan South Korea Poland Portugal
Singapore Switzerland Thailand Turkey Ukraine Vietnam

Oxford is a registered trade mark of Oxford University Press
in the UK and in certain other countries

Text © John Foster 2004
Illustrations by Melanie Williamson and
Rupert Van Wyck

© Oxford University Press 2005

British Library Cataloguing in Publication Data

Data available

ISBN: 978 0 19 911683 6 paperback
7 9 10 8 6
ISBN: 978 0 19 911873 1 hardback
3 5 7 9 10 8 6 4

Typeset in Great Britain by Macwiz

Printed in Malaysia

Paper used in the production of this book is a natural, recyclable product made from wood
grown in sustainable forests. The manufacturing process conforms to the environmental regulations
of the country of origin.

www.schooldictionaries.co.uk

Oxford Junior Rhyming Dictionary

John Foster

Illustrated by Melanie Williamson & Rupert Van Wyk

OXFORD
UNIVERSITY PRESS

How to use this dictionary

You can use this dictionary to help you to find words that rhyme. When you want to find the rhymes for a particular word, the A-Z index on page 146 will help you to find the right page in the dictionary.

You can also use the dictionary to learn how to spell words that belong to the same rhyming family. You will find an index of rhyming sounds on page 143.

The alphabet

The key words in this dictionary are listed in alphabetical order.
There is an alphabet line down the side of each page to help you to find your way round the dictionary.

Key words

A key word is a word that you use very often. In this dictionary, the key words are in **bold**. You can look up a key word and find a list of other words that rhyme with it.

Rhyme family

A rhyme family is a family of words that end with the same rhyming sound and have the same spelling pattern.

Each key word belongs to a rhyme family. You will find the rhyming sound after the key word.

Example

key word

rhyming sound

hole

-ole

rhyme family

mole   pole   role   sole   stole   vole   whole

Sometimes there are several words from one rhyme family which rhyme with words from another rhyme family.

Example

-ole rhymes with -oal
coal   foal   goal

-ole also rhymes with -oll
poll   roll   scroll   stroll   troll

And sometimes there are words that rhyme with the key word but have a different spelling pattern

Example

Other words that rhyme with *mole*

bowl   soul

Rhymes

There are lots of rhymes throughout the dictionary. You can use these rhymes as a starting point for rhymes of your own.

A jaguar from Zanzibar
Learned to sing and to play the guitar.
Now he's a famous movie star
And drives around in a sports car.

Indexes

The dictionary has two indexes. The A-Z index on page 146 lists every word in this dictionary. The key words are printed in bold type. This index will tell you the page where you will find the rhyming words you are looking for.

The Index of Rhyming Sounds on page 143 lists every rhyming sound in this dictionary. You can look up the sound that you want to make rhymes with and go straight to the key word in the main part of the book.

Activities

There is an activities section on page 130. These suggest things you can do to practise making up rhymes and writing rhyming poems.

These are the features of the dictionary:

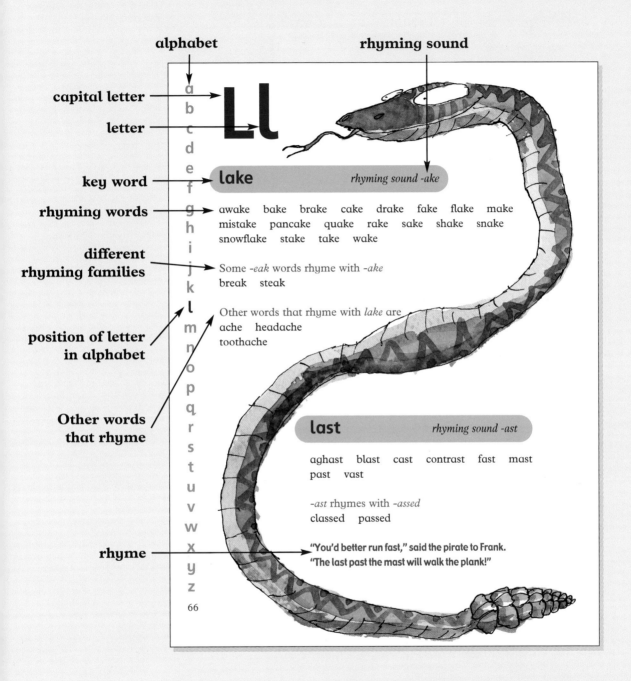

alphabet

rhyming sound

capital letter

letter

key word → lake   *rhyming sound -ake*

rhyming words → awake   bake   brake   cake   drake   fake   flake   make
mistake   pancake   quake   rake   sake   shake   snake
snowflake   stake   take   wake

different rhyming families → Some *-eak* words rhyme with *-ake*
break   steak

Other words that rhyme with *lake* are
ache   headache
toothache

position of letter in alphabet

Other words that rhyme

last   *rhyming sound -ast*

aghast   blast   cast   contrast   fast   mast
past   vast

-ast rhymes with *-assed*
classed   passed

rhyme → "You'd better run fast," said the pirate to Frank.
"The last past the mast will walk the plank!"

66

a b c d e f g h i j k l m n o p q r s t u v w x y z

7

Aa

act
rhyming sound -act

abstract   attract   compact   contact   contract   distract
exact   extract   fact   impact   pact   react   subtract   tact

-act rhymes with *-acked*
backed   backpacked   backtracked   cracked   hijacked
humpbacked   lacked   packed   quacked   sacked   smacked
snacked   stacked   tracked   unpacked   whacked

air
rhyming sound -air

chair   despair   fair   flair   hair   lair   mid-air   pair
repair   stair   unfair

-air rhymes with *-are*
aware   bare   beware   blare   care   compare   dare   declare
fare   glare   hare   mare   nightmare   prepare   rare   scare
share   snare   software   spare   square   stare

-air rhymes with *-aire*
billionaire   millionaire   solitaire

Other words that rhyme with *air*
bear   pear   prayer   swear   their
there   wear   where

Ride on the Ghost Train if you dare.
Feel the spiders as they brush your hair.
Shiver at the gleaming eyes that stare.
Cringe as you pass the vampire's lair.

Ride on the Ghost Train **if you dare!**

a b c d e f g h i j k l m n o p q r s t u v w x y z

9

ant   *rhyming sound -ant*

currant   descendant   elegant   elephant   pant
rant   restaurant   scant

arm   *rhyming sound -arm*

alarm   charm   farm   harm

-arm rhymes with *-alm*
calm   palm

ask   *rhyming sound -ask*

bask   cask   flask   mask   task

Bb

bang   *rhyming sound -ang*

boomerang   clang   fang   gang   hang
overhang   pang   rang   sang   slang
sprang   tang   twang

As the midnight bell rang,
The werewolf bared its fang
And **sprang**.

bank   *rhyming sound -ank*

blank   clank   crank   dank   drank   frank
lank   plank   prank   rank   sank   shrank
spank   stank   tank   thank   yank

beach   *rhyming sound -each*

bleach   each   peach   preach   reach   teach

-each rhymes with *-eech*
beech   screech   speech

My sister gave a loud **screech**
As she bit through the slug in her peach.

a
b
c
d
e
f
g
h
i
j
k
l
m
n
o
p
q
r
s
t
u
v
w
x
y
z

belt *rhyming sound -elt*

celt   dwelt   felt   knelt   melt   pelt
spelt   welt

Another word that rhymes with *belt* is
dealt

big *rhyming sound -ig*

dig   earwig   fig   gig   jig   oil rig   pig
rig   sprig   swig   twig   whirligig   wig

bike *rhyming sound -ike*

alike   dislike   hike   like   pike   spike   strike   trike

bird *rhyming sound -ird*

ladybird   third

Other words that rhyme with *bird*
absurd   blurred   heard   herd   nerd   preferred
purred   stirred   whirred   word

black   *rhyming sound -ack*

attack   back   backpack   bareback   crack   flapjack
hack   haystack   horseback   jack   knack
lack   lumberjack   pack   piggyback
quack   rack   rucksack   sack
shack   slack   smack   snack
soundtrack   stack   tack
track   unpack   whack

Other words that rhyme
with *black*
anorak   kayak   mac   maniac
plaque   tarmac   yak

Mr Black, Mr Black,
Please can we have our
       football back?
You can pass it through
       the window.
It'll fit through the crack.
Oh, don't be a spoilsport, Mr Black.
Please give us our football back.

bone

rhyming sound -one

alone   clone   cone   drone   lone   megaphone   ozone   phone
postpone   prone   stone   timezone   throne   tombstone   tone
trombone   xylophone   zone

-one also rhymes with *-own*
blown   flown   grown   known   own   shown   sown   thrown

Other words which rhyme with *bone*
groan   loan   moan   sewn

"I feel ill," said the king and gave a groan,
when he saw the bill for his mobile phone.

boot

rhyming sound -oot

beetroot hoot loot reboot root
scoot shoot toot

-oot also rhymes with *-ute*
acute brute chutc cute dilute dispute execute flute
minute mute parachute pollute salute substitute

Other words that rhyme with *boot*
fruit newt suit

An elephant in a parachute.

A koala bear playing the flute.

A penguin whizzing down a chute.

And a hippopotamus in a suit.

boss — *rhyming sound -oss*

across   albatross   candyfloss   cross   floss
gloss   loss   moss   toss

bounce — *rhyming sound -ounce*

announce   flounce   ounce   pounce   pronounce
trounce

bridge — *rhyming sound -idge*

fridge   midge
porridge   ridge

*Oh dear! I'm in trouble.
I shouldn't have blown
that bubblegum bubble!*

brother
rhyming sound -other

another   mother   other   smother

bubble
rhyming sound -ubble

rubble   stubble

-ubble also rhymes with *-ouble*
double   trouble

Cc

car
rhyming sound -ar

afar   ajar   bar   caviar   cigar   far   guitar   jaguar
jar   scar   spar   star   tar   tsar

Other words that rhyme with *car*
are   aha   baa   bizarre   ha   ha-ha   ma   pa

A jaguar from Zanzibar
Learned to play the bass guitar.
Now he's a famous movie star
And drives round in a racing car!

cart *rhyming sound -art*

apart art chart dart depart heart part
smart start tart

catch *rhyming sound -atch*

attach batch detach hatch latch match
mis-match patch scratch snatch thatch

cave

rhyming sound -ave

behave   brave   crave   forgave   gave   grave
heatwave   knave   microwave   pave   rave   save   shave
shockwave   slave   wave

"Behave!" said the queen to the knave.
"Or you'll drive me to an early grave!"

coat

rhyming sound -oat

afloat   boat   float   gloat   goat   moat   oat
stoat   throat

-oat rhymes with *-ote*
devote   dote   note   promote   quote
remote   rote   vote   wrote

cook   *rhyming sound -ook*

book   brook   crook   hook   look   mistook   nook   rook
shook   took

My hands shook
When I saw the evil look
In the eyes of Captain Hook
As he **leapt** from the
page of my book.

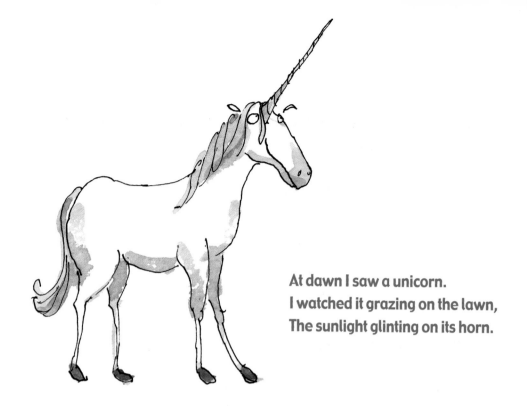

At dawn I saw a unicorn.
I watched it grazing on the lawn,
The sunlight glinting on its horn.

corn   *rhyming sound -orn*

acorn   adorn   born   forlorn   horn   morn   scorn
shorn   sworn   thorn   torn   unicorn   worn

-orn rhymes with *-awn*
airborne   borne   dawn   drawn   fawn   frogspawn
lawn   leprechaun   pawn   sawn   yawn

cow
rhyming sound -ow

allow   bow   bow-wow   brow   eyebrow   how   meow   now
ow!   pow   row   sow   vow   wow

-ow rhymes with some words ending in *-ough*
bough   plough

crab
rhyming sound -ab

cab   dab   drab   fab   flab   grab   jab   kebab   lab
nab   scab   slab   stab

You mustn't try to grab
A very bad–tempered crab.
For if you do,
I'm telling you,
Its pincers will give you a jab.

Anon

a
b
c
d
e
f
g
h
i
j
k
l
m
n
o
p
q
r
s
t
u
v
w
x
y
z

23

crash

rhyming sound -ash

ash   bash   cash   clash   dash   flash   gash   gnash   hash
lash   mash   rash   sash   slapdash   slash   smash   splash
thrash   trash   whiplash

Lightning flash

Thunder crash

Winds lash

Trees thrash

Raindrops splash

Storms smash!

crept
rhyming sound -ept

accept   adept   except   inept   intercept   kept   slept
swept   wept

Other words that rhyme with *crept*
leapt   stepped

I slept in, so I **crept in,**
But Miss saw me, so I was kept in.

Dd

dad

rhyming sound -ad

bad   clad   fad   glad   had   lad   mad
nomad   pad   sad

Another word that rhymes with *dad* is
add

"You're not a bad lad," said dad.
"But your music drives me **mad**!"

dance

rhyming sound -ance

advance   chance   entrance   France   glance   lance
prance   stance   trance

dark

rhyming sound -ark

aardvark ark bark embark hark landmark
lark mark park remark shark spark

"My bite is worse than my bark," said the shark.
"With my teeth I leave my mark!"

a b c d e f g h i j k l m n o p q r s t u v w x y z

28

dinner
rhyming sound -inner

beginner   inner   sinner   spinner
thinner   winner

dog
rhyming sound -og

agog   bog   clog   cog   flog   fog   frog   grog
hog   jog   log   slog

-og also rhymes with *-ogue*
catalogue   monologue

dream
rhyming sound -eam

beam   cream   daydream   gleam
ice cream   scream   seam   steam
stream   team

-eam also rhymes with *-eem*
redeem   seem   teem

Other words that rhyme with *dream*
extreme   scheme   supreme   theme

dress   *rhyming sound -ess*

address   bless   chess   confess   cress   depress   distress
excess   express   guess   happiness   helpless   impress
kindness   less   loneliness   mess   oppress   possess   press
princess   progress   stress   success   tress   unless

Another word that rhymes with *dress* is
yes

Nicola Nicholas couldn't care less.
Nicola Nicholas tore her dress.
Nicola Nicholas tore her knickers.
Now Nicola Nicholas is knickerless.

duck   *rhyming sound -uck*

buck   chuck   cluck   luck   muck   pluck
struck   stuck   suck   truck   tuck   yuck

dust   *rhyming sound -ust*

adjust   bust   crust   disgust
gust   just   must   rust
thrust   trust

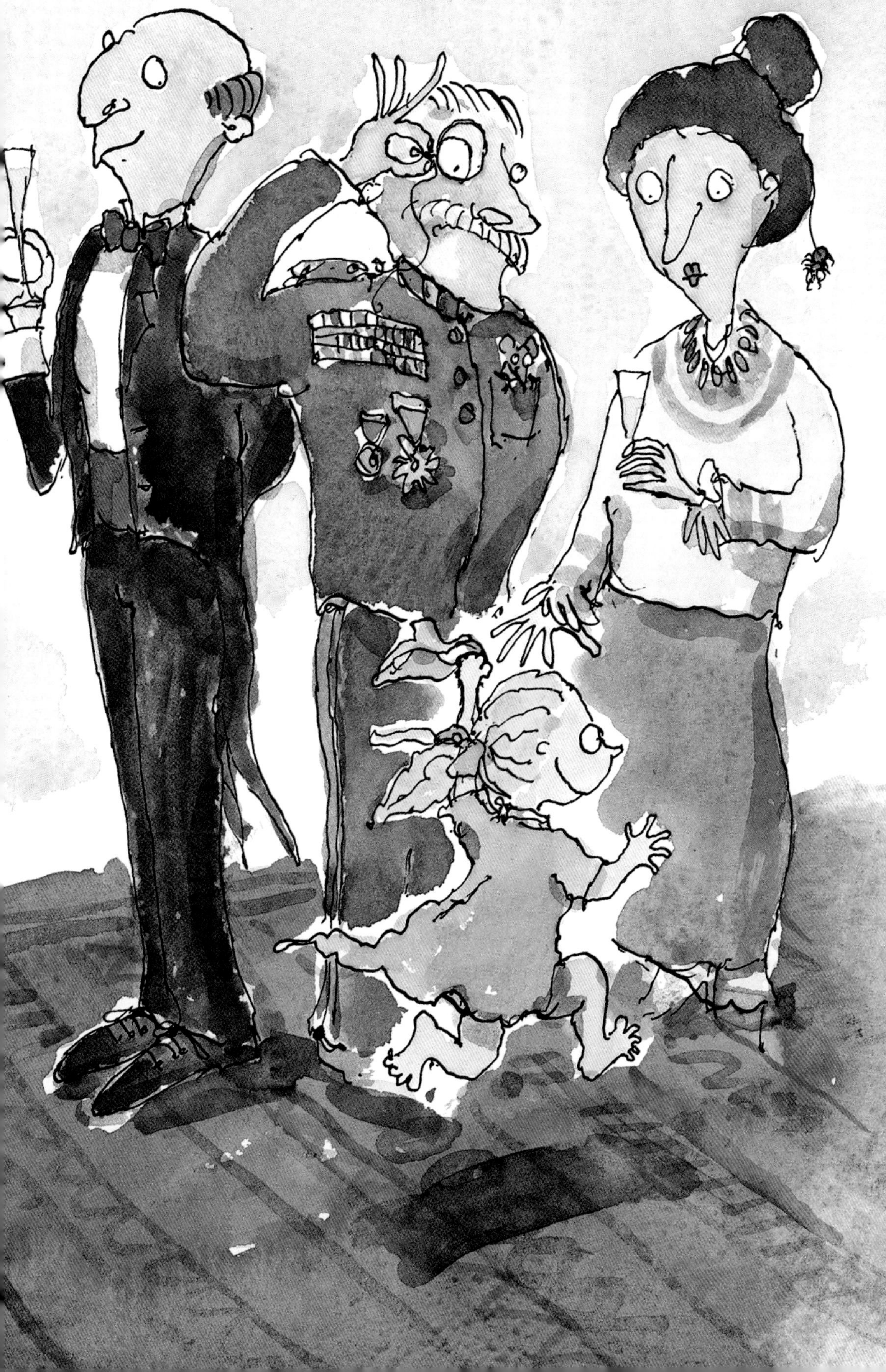

a b c d **e** f g h i j k l m n o p q r s t u v w x y z

Ee

ear   *rhyming sound -ear*

appear   clear   dear   disappear   fear
gear   hear   near   rear   shear   smear
spear   tear

-ear rhymes with *-eer*
beer   buccaneer   career   cheer   deer   engineer   jeer
leer   mountaineer   musketeer   peer   pioneer   sheer
sneer   steer   veer   volunteer

-ear rhymes with *-ere*
atmosphere   here   mere   persevere
revere   severe   sincere

Other words that rhyme with *ear*
cashier   cavalier   frontier   gondolier
pier   souvenir   weir

We all gave a cheer
as the wizard made our teacher
disappear.

32

east
rhyming sound -east

beast   feast   least   yeast

-east rhymes with *-eased*
ceased   creased   deceased   greased
increased   released

elf
rhyming sound -elf

bookshelf   herself   himself   itself
myself   self   shelf   yourself

end
rhyming sound -end

ascend   attend   bend   blend   defend   depend
descend   extend   friend   intend   lend   mend   offend
pretend   recommend   send   spend   suspend   tend   trend

Here lies Charlotte Cul-de-Sac,
A most annoying friend,
She used to drive me round the bend
Until she came to a dead end.

ever
rhyming sound -ever

clever   forever   however   never   sever   whatever
whenever   wherever   whichever   whoever

Ff

face
rhyming sound -ace

ace brace commonplace disgrace embrace
fireplace grace lace misplace pace place
race replace shoelace space trace

-ace also rhymes with *-ase*
base bookcase case chase database
staircase suitcase

There was a young girl called Grace
Whose nose spread all over her face
She had very few kisses
And the reason for this is
There wasn't a suitable place.

Anon

find

rhyming sound -ind

behind   bind   blind   grind   kind   mind   remind
rewind   rind   unkind   wind

-ind rhymes with *-ined*
dined   fined   lined   mined   pined   whined

Another word that rhymes with *find* is
signed

When
you stand
in a
queue,
it's not
kind
to remind
anyone
you're
behind
that
you're
behind
their
behind.

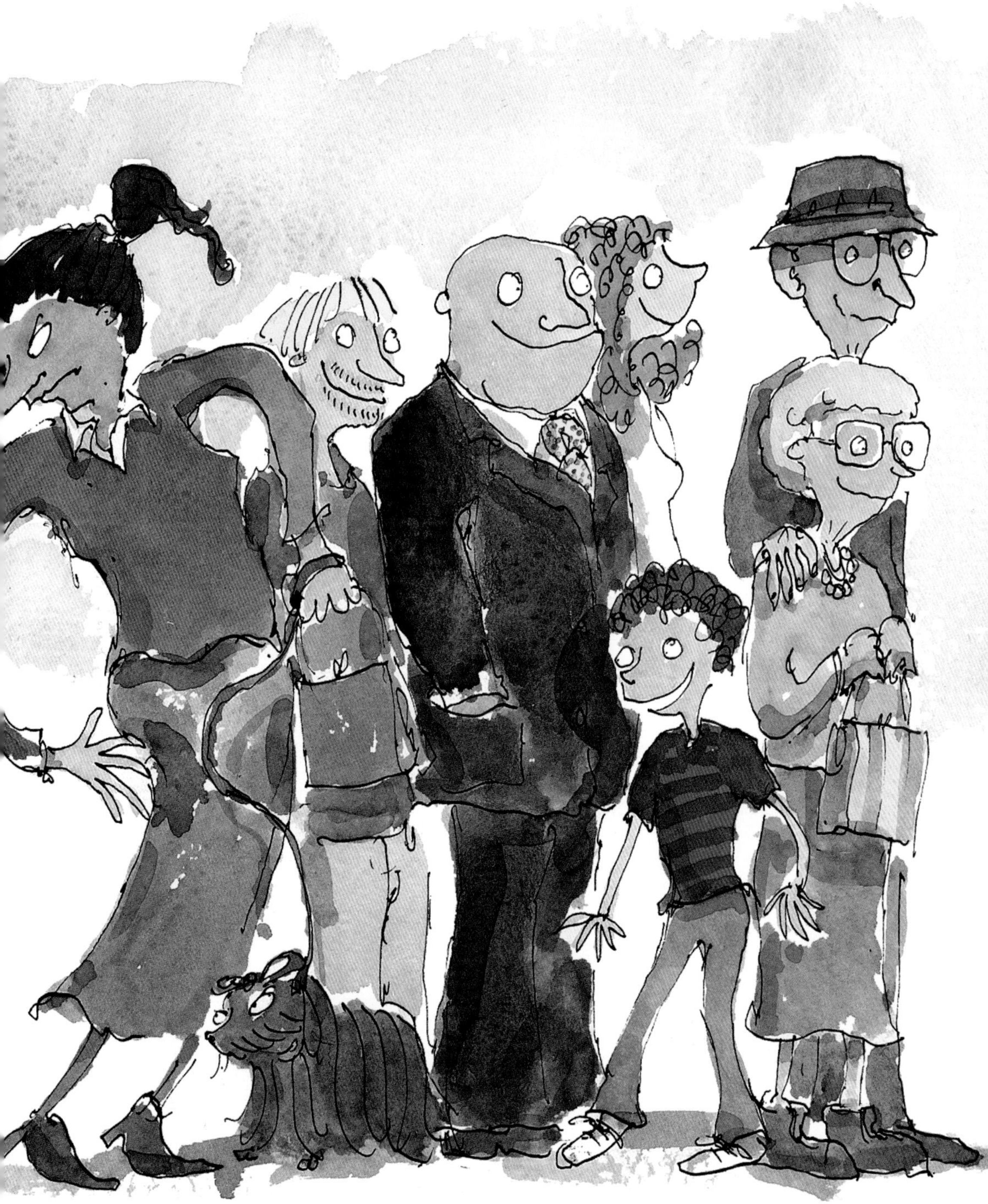

a b c d e f g h i j k l m n o p q r s t u v w x y z

fire

rhyming sound -ire

admire   bonfire   desire   dire   empire   hire   inquire   inspire
quagmire   spire   squire   tire   umpire   vampire   wire

Other words that rhyme with *fire*
choir   flyer   friar   fryer   higher
liar   pyre   tyre

Here lies a foolish young squire
Who was the most terrible liar.
He collapsed one day
And passed away
From the heat of his pants on fire!

first
rhyming sound -irst

thirst

Other words that rhyme with *first*
burst   cursed   nursed   rehearsed   worst

fish
rhyming sound -ish

dish   perish   punish   rubbish   selfish
squish   swish   vanish   wish

**Three selfish shellfish each had a wish.
The wish each selfish shellfish wished
was a selfish shellfish wish.**

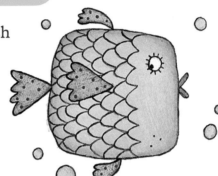

five
rhyming sound -ive

alive   arrive   dive   drive   hive   jive   live   revive
strive   survive

Another word that thymes with *five* is
I've

flag
rhyming sound -ag

bag   brag   crag   drag   gag   hag   lag   nag   rag
sag   snag   stag   swag   tag   wag   zigzag

a
b
c
d
e
f
g
h
i
j
k
l
m
n
o
p
q
r
s
t
u
v
w
x
y
z

food
rhyming sound -ood

brood   mood

-ood also rhymes with *-ewed*
brewed   chewed   mewed   screwed   slewed   viewed

-ood also rhymes with *-ooed*
booed   boo-hooed   cooed   mooed   shampooed   shooed
tattooed   wooed

-ood also rhymes with *-ude*
altitude   attitude   crude
exclude
gratitude   include
intrude   nude   rude
solitude

-ood also rhymes
with *-ued*
argued
barbecued   glued
pursued
rescued   sued

40

fox

box   cox   ox   pox

-ox rhymes with *-ocks*

blocks   clocks   docks   flocks   frocks   knocks   locks   mocks
rocks   shocks   socks   stocks

Goldilocks wears pretty frocks
But I wish she'd change her   smelly socks.

freeze   *rhyming sound -eeze*

breeze   sneeze   squeeze   wheeze

-eeze rhymes with *-ees*
agrees   bees   chimpanzees   degrees   dungarees   fees
flees   frees   knees   referees   sees   toffees   trees

-eeze also rhymes with *-ease*
disease   ease   please   tease

Other words that rhyme with *-eeze*
cheese   chimneys   donkeys   fleas   keys   monkeys
peas   seas   seize   skis   teas   these   trapeze

Chimpanzees in dungarees
Swing with ease on the trapeze,
While bees on skis
Struggle to juggle packs of peas.

a
b
c
d
e
f
g
h
i
j
k
l
m
n
o
p
q
r
s
t
u
v
w
x
y
z

43

fur

rhyming sound -ur

blur   occur   slur
spur

-ur rhymes with *-ir*
fir   sir   stir

-ur also rhymes with *-er*
badger   her   otter
prefer   slipper   tiger

Other words that rhyme with *fur*
purr   were   whirr

Always call a tiger "Sir"
And do not try to stroke his fur
For tigers are well known to Grrr!

Gg

gate *rhyming sound -ate*

appreciate   ate   calculate   celebrate   concentrate   confiscate
crate   create   date   debate   decorate   educate   estate
estimate   exaggerate   fascinate   fate   frustrate   grate   hate
investigate   irritate   Kate   late   mate   operate   plate   rate
separate   skate   slate   state

-ate also rhymes with *-ait*
bait   wait

Other words that rhyme with *gate*
eight   fete   great   straight   weight

Elephant! Elephant!
Don't try to skate.
The ice is too thin,
It won't bear your
weight...

Too late!

a b c d e f **g** h i j k l m n o p q r s t u v w x y z

girl
rhyming sound -irl

swirl   twirl   whirl

-irl rhymes with *-url*
curl   furl   hurl   unfurl

Other words that rhyme with *girl*
earl   pearl

glass
rhyming sound -ass

brass   bypass   class   grass   pass   trespass

grape
rhyming sound -ape

agape   ape   cape   drape   escape   gape
landscape   scrape   shape   tape

grub

rhyming sound -ub

club   cub   dub   hub   hubbub   pub   rub   scrub   shrub
snub   stub   tub

A grubby grub sat in a tub
And sang as he had a good scrub:

"I'm a scrub-a-grub, rub-a-dub grub!"

Hh

hairy   *rhyming sound -airy*

airy   dairy   fairy

-airy rhymes with *-ary*
canary   contrary   Mary   scary   vary   wary

hand   *rhyming sound -and*

and   band   brand   expand   gland   grand   land
sand   stand   strand   understand

-and rhymes with *-anned*
banned   canned   fanned   manned   planned
scanned   spanned   tanned

hat
rhyming sound -at

acrobat   aristocrat   at   bat   brat   cat   chat   combat   fat flat   gnat   habitat   mat   pat   pit-a-pat   rat   rat-a-tat-tat sat   spat   splat   that   vat   wombat

There was a young fellow called Matt
Who wanted to look like a cat
His feet were like paws
With retractable claws
And whiskers grew out of his hat.

Anon

hen
rhyming sound -en

amen   Ben   den   fen   glen   Ken   Len   men pen   ten   then   when   wren   yen

Another word that rhymes with *hen* is again

hit
rhyming sound -it

admit   bandit   biscuit   bit   circuit   culprit   exit   fit   flit grit   habit   it   kit   knit   lit   nit   omit   orbit   outfit   permit pit   quit   rabbit   sit   spit   split   summit   twit   visit   wit

a b c d e f g h i j k l m n o p q r s t u v w x y z

hole

rhyming sound -ole

casserole   console   dole   mole   pole   role
sole   stole   tadpole   vole   whole

-ole rhymes with *-oal*
coal   foal   goal   shoal

-ole also rhymes with *-oll*
poll   roll   scroll   stroll   troll

Other words that rhyme with *hole*
bowl   control   soul

Old King Cole scored a very fine goal
A very fine goal scored he.
A TV poll reckoned King Cole's goal
Was the best you'd ever see.

a b c d e f **g** h **i** j k l m n o p **q** r s t u v w x y z

honey

rhyming sound -oney

money

-oney rhymes with *-unny*

bunny   funny   runny   sunny

I eat my peas with honey.
I've done it all my life.
It makes the peas taste funny.
But it keeps them on the knife.

Anon

a b c d e f g h i j k l m n o p q r s t u v w x y z

a b c d e f g h i j k l m n o p q r s t u v w x y z

a
b
c
d
e
f
g
h
i
j
k
l
m
n
o
p
q
r
s
t
u
v
w
x
y
z

hood

rhyming sound -ood

childhood   deadwood   driftwood   falsehood   good
neighbourhood   stood   understood   wood

-ood rhymes with *-ould*
could   should   would

hoop

rhyming sound -oop

coop   droop   loop   nincompoop
scoop   sloop   snoop   stoop
swoop   troop   whoop

-oop rhymes with *-oup*
group   soup

house

rhyming sound -ouse

louse   mouse   spouse

A mouse and his spouse doing cartwheels round the house.

54

hunt
rhyming sound -unt

blunt   grunt   punt   runt   shunt   stunt

Another word that rhymes with *hunt* is
front

hut
rhyming sound -ut

but   chestnut   cut   doughnut   glut   gut
jut   nut   rut   shut   strut   tut-tut

Another word that rhymes
with *hut* is
putt

Ii

ice
rhyming sound -ice

advice   dice   lice   mice   nice   price   rice   sacrifice   slice
spice   splice   trice   twice   vice

The three blind mice said,
"It's not very nice
Of the farmer's wife
To want to slice
Our tails off with her carving knife!"

Other words that
rhyme with *ice*
paradise
precise

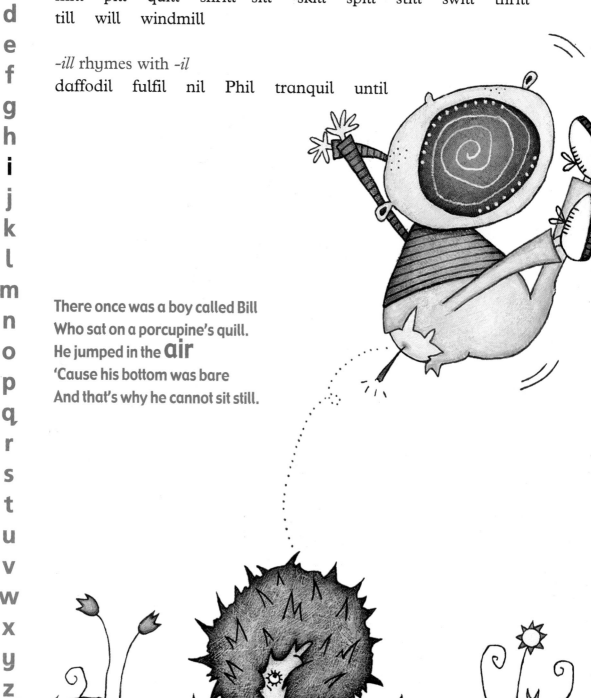

ill

rhyming sound -ill

bill   brill   chill   drill   fill   frill   gill   grill   hill   Jill   kill
mill   pill   quill   shrill   sill   skill   spill   still   swill   thrill
till   will   windmill

-ill rhymes with *-il*
daffodil   fulfil   nil   Phil   tranquil   until

There once was a boy called Bill
Who sat on a porcupine's quill.
He jumped in the **air**
'Cause his bottom was bare
And that's why he cannot sit still.

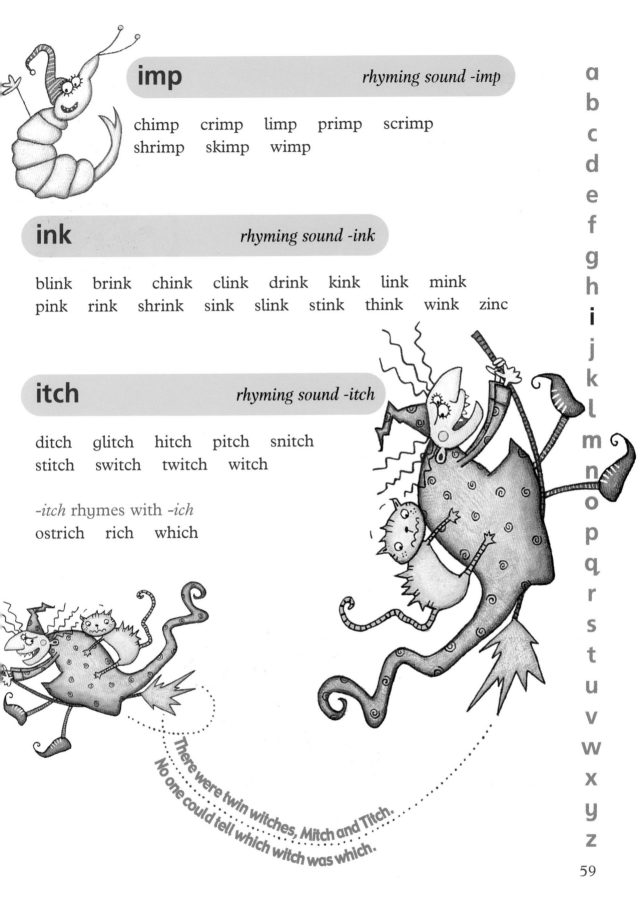

imp
rhyming sound -imp

chimp crimp limp primp scrimp
shrimp skimp wimp

ink
rhyming sound -ink

blink brink chink clink drink kink link mink
pink rink shrink sink slink stink think wink zinc

itch
rhyming sound -itch

ditch glitch hitch pitch snitch
stitch switch twitch witch

-itch rhymes with *-ich*
ostrich rich which

a
b
c
d
e
f
g
h
i
j
k
l
m
n
o
p
q
r
s
t
u
v
w
x
y
z

There were twin witches, Mitch and Titch.
No one could tell which witch was which.

59

Jj

jam *rhyming sound -am*

am cram dam exam gram ham
Pam pram program ram Sam scam
scram sham slam swam tram wham
wigwam yam

Another word that rhymes with *jam* is
lamb

jet *rhyming sound -et*

alphabet basket bet bracelet bucket carpet clarinet
cricket duet fidget forget fret gadget get helmet
internet jacket let magnet met net pet pocket
puppet regret rocket secret set ticket trumpet upset
vet wet yet

-et also rhymes with *-eat*
sweat threat

-et also rhymes with *-ette*
baguette cassette courgette launderette
omelette serviette

Another word that rhymes with *jet* is

debt

job
rhyming sound -ob

blob   bob   cob   gob   hob   hobnob   knob   lob   mob
rob   snob   sob   throb

jug
rhyming sound -ug

bug   chug   drug   dug   glug   hug   humbug   lug   mug
plug   rug   shrug   slug   smug   snug   thug   tug

A slimy slug drank from a jug.
A grubby bug drank from a mug.

Then the slug gave the *bug* a *hug!*

jump
rhyming sound -ump

bump   clump   dump   frump   goosebump   hump
lump   plump   pump   rump   slump   stump
thump   trump

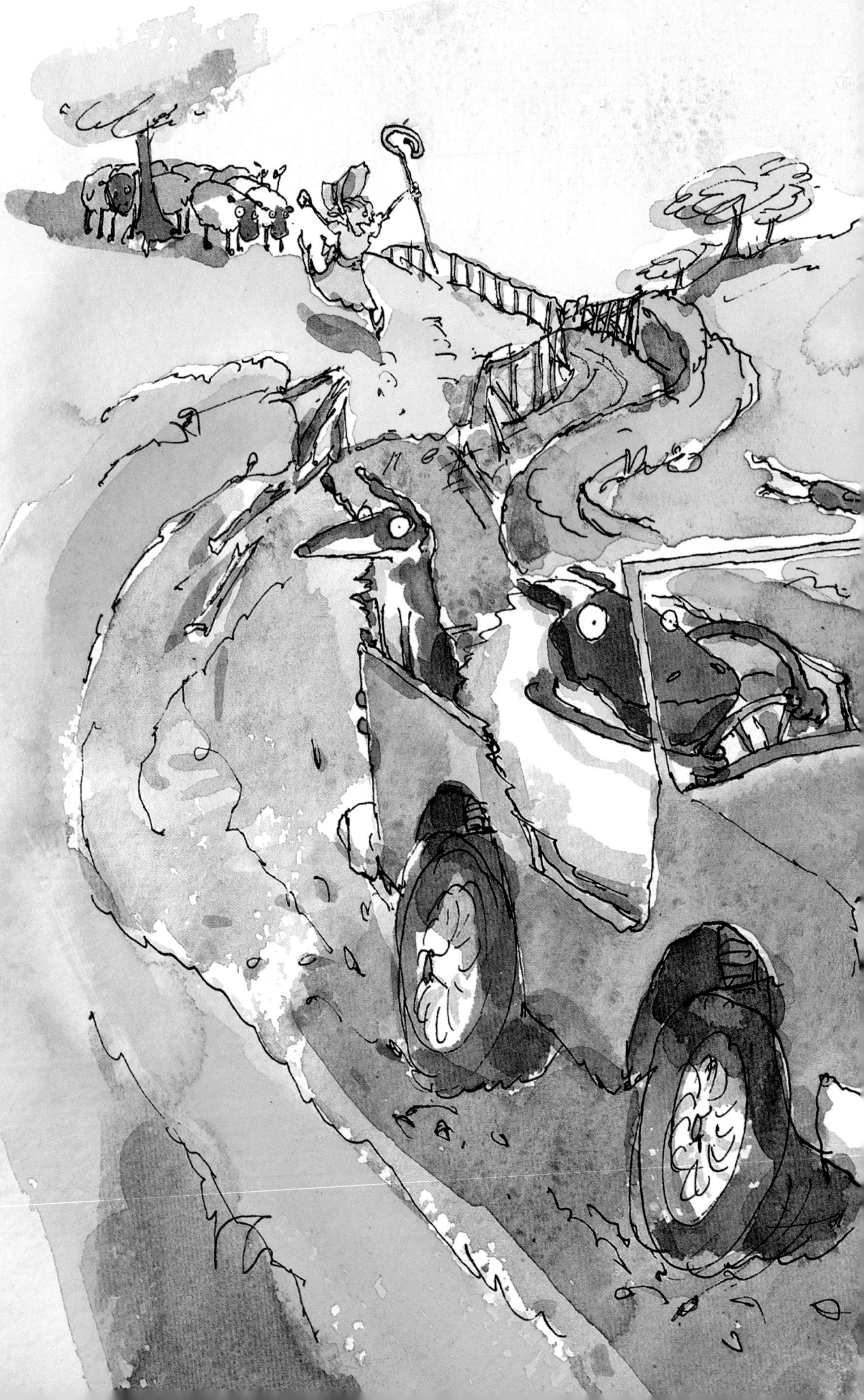

Kk

keep
rhyming sound -eep

asleep beep bleep cheep creep deep jeep
peep seep sheep sleep steep sweep weep

-eep rhymes with *-eap*
cheap heap leap reap

I'm a runaway sheep.
I stole the keys to Bo Peep's jeep
While she was lying fast asleep
Get out of my way! Beep! Beep!

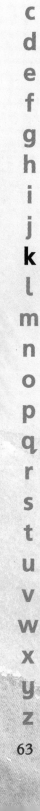

king

rhyming sound -ing

boring bring ceiling cling ding fling ping ring
sing sling spring sting string swing thing wing
wring zing

When the bee gave the king a sting
The king did a highland fling.
So his arm ended up in a sling.

kiss
rhyming sound -iss

amiss   bliss   dismiss   hiss   kiss   miss

Other words that rhyme with *kiss*
liquorice   office   practice   promise   service   this

I'll be good, Mum, just promise me this:
You won't try to give me a kiss
In the playground. Just give it a miss!

knock
rhyming sound -ock

block   clock   crock   dock   flock   frock   lock   mock
rock   shock   sock   stock   tick-tock

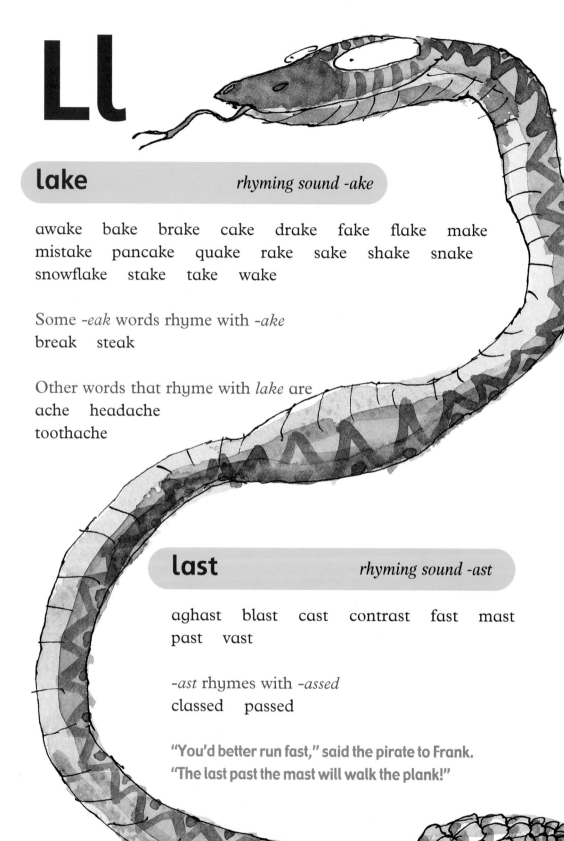

Ll

lake   rhyming sound -ake

awake   bake   brake   cake   drake   fake   flake   make
mistake   pancake   quake   rake   sake   shake   snake
snowflake   stake   take   wake

Some -*eak* words rhyme with -*ake*
break   steak

Other words that rhyme with *lake* are
ache   headache
toothache

last   rhyming sound -ast

aghast   blast   cast   contrast   fast   mast
past   vast

-*ast* rhymes with -*assed*
classed   passed

"You'd better run fast," said the pirate to Frank.
"The last past the mast will walk the plank!"

leg

rhyming sound -eg

beg   dreg   Greg   keg   Meg   nutmeg   peg

Another word that rhymes with *leg* is
egg

lid

rhyming sound -id

bid   did   forbid   grid   hid   liquid   kid   pyramid   quid
rapid   rid   rigid   skid   slid   squid   stupid   timid   undid

I slid back the bolt and undid the locks
To see what lay hid in the secret box.

a
b
c
d
e
f
g
h
i
j
k
l
m
n
o
p
q
r
s
t
u
v
w
x
y
z

light
rhyming sound -ight

bright   delight   fight   flight   fright   knight   midnight
might   night   outright   playwright   plight   right   sight
slight   stagefright   tight   tonight   twilight   upright   uptight

-ight rhymes with *-ite*
appetite   bite   dynamite   excite   ignite   invite   kite   mite
polite   quite   recite   site   spite   sprite   unite   website
white   write

Other words that rhyme with *light*
byte   height

When Dwight Wright had stagefright,
Mrs Wright said, "Don't get uptight, Dwight,
It'll be all right on the night."

After the first night, Dwight Wright
Said, "It went all right.
You were quite right, Mrs Wright."

lord

rhyming sound -ord

afford　chord　cord　ford　record　sword

-ord rhymes with *-oard*
aboard　board　cardboard　hoard　keyboard
scoreboard　skateboard

-ord also rhymes with *-ored*
adored　bored　explored　ignored　scored　snored　stored

Other words that rhyme with *lord*
abroad　applaud　award　broad　horde　poured　reward
roared　soared　toward　ward

The crowd roared and began to applaud
As the young lord drew his sword,
Slew the monster and claimed the reward.

a
b
c
d
e
f
g
h
i
j
k
l
m
n
o
p
q
r
s
t
u
v
w
x
y
z

69

love   *rhyming sound -ove*

above   dove   glove   shove

lunch   *rhyming sound -unch*

brunch   bunch   crunch   hunch   munch   punch   scrunch

lung   *rhyming sound -ung*

bung   clung   dung   flung   hung   rung   slung   sprung
strung   stung   sung   swung   wrung

Other words that rhyme with *lung*
among   tongue   young

Mm

map
rhyming sound -ap

bap   cap   chap   clap   flap   gap   kidnap   lap   nap
overlap   rap   sap   scrap   slap   snap   strap   tap
trap   unwrap   wrap   yap   zap

On the Clip Clop Clap
All the Flops flip flap
And the Bongles boogie in the breeze.
The Sniggers snip snap
The Trotters trip trap
And the Somersaults sniff and sneeze
The Somersaults sniff and sneeze.

meat

rhyming sound -eat

beat   bleat   cheat   defeat   eat   feat   heat   neat
peat   pleat   repeat   retreat   seat   treat   wheat

-eat rhymes with *-eet*
discreet   feet   fleet   greet   meet   parakeet   sheet
sleet   street   sweet

-eat also rhymes with *-ete*
athlete   compete   complete   concrete   delete

Pete dressed up in a sheet
And went round the street
Knocking on doors
Saying, **"Trick or treat?"**

But at number thirty four
Pete got more
Than he bargained for,
When a troll opened the door!

So Pete beat a hasty retreat.

merry
rhyming sound -erry

berry   cherry   ferry   Terry

Other words that rhyme with *merry*
bury   very

middle
rhyming sound -iddle

diddle   fiddle   griddle   riddle   twiddle

Hey diddle riddle
The first is in first
The rest is in middle!

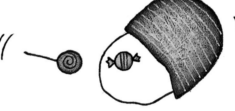

mist   *rhyming sound -ist*

cyclist   fist   insist   list   resist   tourist   twist   wrist

-ist rhymes with *-issed*
dismissed   hissed   kissed   missed

mix   *rhyming sound -ix*

fix   matrix   phoenix   six

-ix rhymes with *-icks*
bricks   broomsticks   chicks   clicks   flicks   gimmicks
kicks   licks   matchsticks   nicks   picks   pricks   sticks
ticks   tricks

The ghost of the conjuror said,
"I'm really in a fix.
The problem is the audience
Sees right through all my tricks."

moon   *rhyming sound -oon*

afternoon   baboon   balloon   bassoon
cartoon   croon   harpoon   honeymoon
lagoon   macaroon   maroon   noon
platoon   raccoon   saloon   soon
spoon   swoon   tycoon   typhoon

A baboon in a saloon playing a tune on a bassoon.

-oon rhymes with *-une*

dune   fortune   June   Neptune   prune   tune

Another word that rhymes with *moon* is
strewn

mud   *rhyming sound -ud*

bud   cud   dud   scud   spud
stud   sud   thud

Other words that rhyme with
mud
blood   flood

mum   *rhyming sound -um*

chum   drum   glum   gum   hum
plum   rum   scrum   scum   slum
strum   sum   swum   tum   yum
yum-yum

-um rhymes with *-umb*

crumb   dumb   numb   plumb   succumb
thumb

Other words that rhyme with *mum*
become   come   some

a
b
c
d
e
f
g
h
i
j
k
l
m
n
o
p
q
r
s
t
u
v
w
x
y
z

75

Nn

name
rhyming sound -ame

became   blame   came   fame   flame   frame   game
lame   same   shame   tame

-ame rhymes with *-aim*
acclaim   aim   claim   exclaim   maim

I am the wizard's dragon.
I speak with tongues of flame.
I am the wizard's dragon.
Firesnorter is my name.

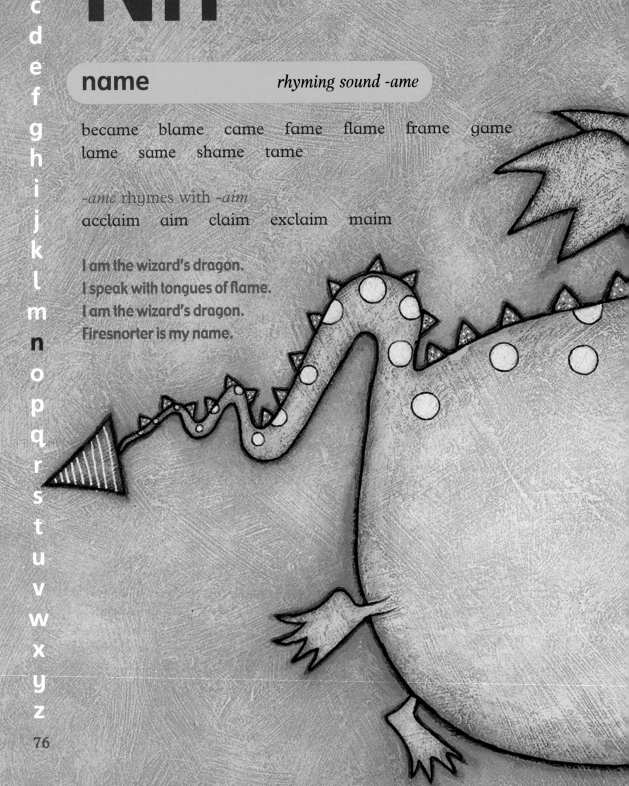

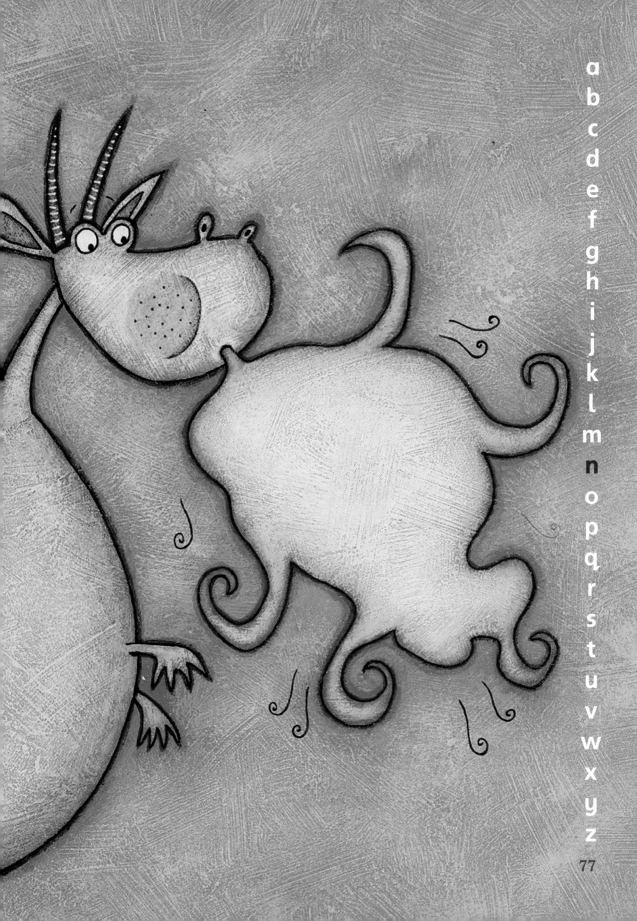

b
c
d
e
f
g
h
i
j
k
l
m
n
o
p
q
r
s
t
u
v
w
x
y
z

neck — *rhyming sound -eck*

beck check deck fleck peck speck wreck

Other words that rhyme with *neck*
cheque Czech discotheque high-tech trek

**"Just let me check," said the vampire.
"I think there's a speck
Of blood on your neck."**

nettle — *rhyming sound -ettle*

fettle kettle settle

-ettle rhymes with *-etal*
metal petal

78

nine

airline   brine   combine   define   dine   divine   fine   line
mine   pine   recline   shine   shrine   spine   swine   twine
valentine   vine   whine   wine

-ine rhymes with *-ign*
design   resign   sign

It sent a shiver down my spine
When I received a valentine,
Saying, "I think you are divine"
'Cause it was signed 'Frankenstein'!

nose · *rhyming sound -ose*

chose close expose hose pose prose propose rose suppose those

-ose rhymes with -ows
arrows bellows blows bows bungalows crows elbows flows glows grows knows meadows mows rows shadows shows slows snows sows stows throws tows

-ose also rhymes with -oes
foes goes hoes toes woes oboes volcanoes tiptoes dominoes potatoes

-ose also rhymes with -os
radios stereos videos

Other words that rhyme with *nose*
bulldoze doze froze sews UFOs

When the winter wind blows
An icicle grows on the scarecrow's nose
And it looks just like Pinnochio's!

Oo

oak   *rhyming sound -oak*

cloak   croak   soak

-oak rhymes with *-oke*
awoke   bloke   broke   choke   coke
joke   poke   provoke   smoke   spoke
stroke   woke   yoke

Other words that rhyme with *oak*
folk   yolk

oil   *rhyming sound -oil*

boil   broil   coil   foil   recoil   soil   spoil
toil   turmoil

-oil rhymes with *-oyal*
loyal   royal

Another word that rhymes
with *oil* is
gargoyle

old

rhyming sound -old

behold   bold   cold   fold   gold   hold   marigold   scaffold
scold   sold   told

Other words that rhyme with *old*
bowled   cajoled   consoled   controlled   mould   patrolled
polled   rolled   soled   strolled

"Behold!" said the wizard
And he conjured a room full of gold.
But my blood ran cold,
When he warned,
"My secrets must never be told."

out
rhyming sound -out

about blackout bout clout dugout hideout knockout lookout lout pout rout scout shootout shout snout spout sprout stout throughout trout without

Other words that rhyme with *out*
doubt drought

owl
rhyming sound -owl

fowl growl howl prowl scowl yowl

-owl rhymes with *-owel*
bowel towel trowel vowel

Another word that rhymes
with *owl* is
foul

Pp

page
rhyming sound -age

age   cage   engage   enrage   outrage   rage
rampage   sage   stage   teenage   upstage   wage

"It's like being on stage.
Let me out or pay me a wage!"
The monkey screeched in a rage
As it rattled the bars of its cage.

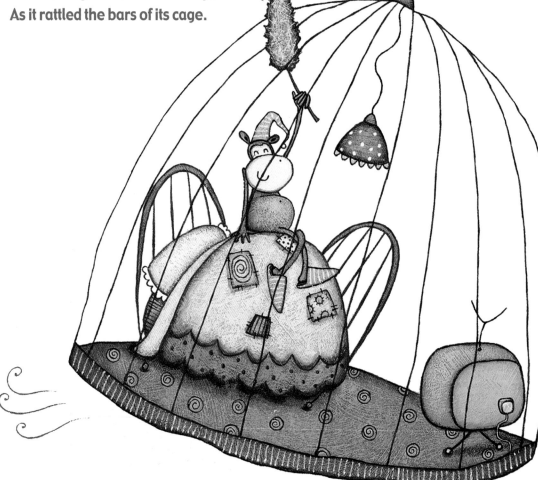

paint
rhyming sound -aint

complaint   faint   quaint   saint   taint

paste
rhyming sound -aste

haste   taste   waste

-aste rhymes with *-aced*
braced   disgraced   embraced   faced   graced   laced   paced
placed   raced   replaced   spaced   traced

Other words that rhyme with *paste*
chased   waist

pond
rhyming sound -ond

beyond   blond   bond   fond   respond

Another word that rhymes with *pond* is
wand

Said the frog in the pond,
"Please kiss me or wave your wand."
But the princess didn't respond.

pool *rhyming sound -ool*

cool drool fool school spool stool
toadstool tool whirlpool

-ool rhymes with *-ule*
capsule globule miniscule molecule
mule ridicule rule schedule yule

Other words that rhyme with *pool*
fuel ghoul

**In our school
There's an empty stool
Where nobody sits
Except the ghoul
Of the pupil who died
While playing the fool.**

post *rhyming sound -ost*

almost ghost host most
signpost utmost

-ost rhymes with *-oast*
boast coast
roast toast

**At the Halloween Ball
Our host was a ghost
Who walked through the wall.**

pot

rhyming sound -ot

apricot   blot   cannot   clot   cot   dot   earshot   forgot   got
hot   jackpot   jot   knot   lot   mascot   not   plot   robot   rot
Scot   shot   slot   snot   spot   swot   tot   trot

Other words that rhyme with *pot*
squat   swat   what   yacht

Ned Nott was shot
And Sam Shott was not.
So it's better to be Shott than Nott.

Anon

print

rhyming sound -int

flint   footprint   glint
hint   lint   mint
skint   splint   sprint
squint   tint

puff
rhyming sound -uff

bluff   buff   cuff   dandruff   duff   fluff   gruff   handcuff
huff   scruff   scuff   snuff   stuff

Some *-ough* words rhyme with *puff*
enough   rough   tough

pull
rhyming sound -ull

bull   full

-ull rhymes with *-ul*
armful   awful   beautiful   careful   cheerful   doubtful
dreadful   faithful   fearful   graceful   harmful   hopeful
joyful   playful   useful   wonderful

Another word that rhymes with *pull* is
wool

Qq

queen
rhyming sound -een

been   between   canteen   green   keen   preen   screen   seen
sheen   spleen   teen   thirteen   fourteen (etc)

-een rhymes with *-ean*
bean   clean   glean   Jean   lean   mean   wean

-een also rhymes with *-ine*
limousine   magazine   routine   sardine   tangerine   trampoline

-een also rhymes with *-ene*
gene   hygiene   scene   serene

"I'm a queen," said Kathleen.
"We've been filming a scene.
That's my picture in a magazine
And over there's my limousine."
"Dream on," said Jean.

quick
rhyming sound -ick

brick   chick   click   flick   gimmick   kick   lick   limerick
pick   prick   sick   slick   stick   thick   tick   trick   wick

-ick rhymes with *-ic*
attic   basic   comic   elastic   electric   fantastic   frantic
garlic   lunatic   magic   music   panic   picnic   plastic   public
supersonic   terrific   tragic

Rr

rain
rhyming sound -ain

again   brain   chain   complain   contain   drain   entertain
explain   gain   grain   main   obtain   pain   plain   refrain
remain   Spain   sprain   stain   strain   train   vain

-ain rhymes with *-ane*
cane   crane   Jane   lane   mane   pane   plane   sane   vane

Other words that rhyme with *rain*
rein   vein   reign

There was a young girl called Elaine
Who was dreadfully sick on the train –
Not once but again and again!

red

bed bled bred fed fled led moped quadruped red
shed shred sled sped Ted wed

-ed words rhyme with some *-ead* words
ahead bread dead dread head instead lead read
spread thread tread widespread

Another word that rhymes with *red* is
said

"I sped down the hill on my sled,
But I crashed and demolished the shed,"
Said Ted, as he lay on the bed
Feeling the bump on his head.

a b c d e f g h i j k l m n o p q r s t u v w x y z

ride

rhyming sound -ide

aside astride beside bride collide countryside decide divide glide guide hide inside pride provide side slide stride tide wide

-ide rhymes with *-ied*
cried defied denied died dried fried horrified lied spied terrified tied tried

Other words that rhyme with *ride*
dyed eyed I'd sighed

river

rhyming sound -iver

deliver   liver   quiver   shiver   sliver

It made me shake.
It made me shiver.
When the highwayman's ghost

Shouted,
"Stand and deliver!"

a
b
c
d
e
f
g
h
i
j
k
l
m
n
o
p
q
r
s
t
u
v
w
x
y
z

road

rhyming sound -oad

goad   load   toad

-oad rhymes with *-ode*
code   episode   erode   explode   mode   ode   rode   strode

-oad also rhymes with *-owed*
burrowed   crowed   flowed   glowed   mowed   owed   rowed
showed   slowed   snowed   stowed   towed

Here lies the body of a toad.
Who forgot his Highway Code.
And didn't wait till the traffic slowed,
Before he tried to cross the road.

room
rhyming sound -oom

bloom   boom   bridegroom   broom   doom   gloom   groom
heirloom   loom   mushroom   zoom

-oom rhymes with *-ume*
costume   flume   fume   perfume   plume

Other words that rhyme with *room*
tomb   whom   womb

A skeleton once in Khartoum
Invited a ghost to his room
They spent the whole night
In the eeriest fight
As to who should be frightened of whom.

Anon

rope   *rhyming sound -ope*

antelope   cope   dope   elope   envelope   grope   hope
horoscope   lope   microscope   mope   pope   scope   slope
telescope   tightrope

Another word that rhymes with *rope* is
soap

**"I hope I can cope," said the antelope
as it started to walk along the tightrope.**

round   *rhyming sound -ound*

around   astound   background   bound
found   ground   hound   mound   pound
profound   sound   surround   wound

-ound rhymes with *-owned*
browned   clowned   crowned   downed   drowned
frowned   renowned

**My heart begins to pound
As I spin round and round,
On the whirling, twirling wheel
And I wish I was on the ground!**

rumble   *rhyming sound -umble*

bumble   crumble   fumble   grumble
humble   jumble   mumble   stumble   tumble

rush

rhyming sound -ush

blush   brush   crush   flush   gush   hush   lush   mush
plush   shush   slush   thrush

Ss

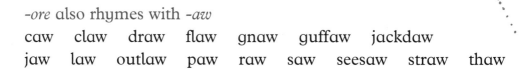

score

rhyming sound -ore

adore   ashore   before   bore   carnivore   chore   core   encore
explore   galore   gore   ignore   more   ore   pore   shore
snore   sore   store   swore   therefore   tore   wore

-ore rhymes with *-oar*
boar   oar   roar   soar

-ore also rhymes with *-aw*
caw   claw   draw   flaw   gnaw   guffaw   jackdaw
jaw   law   outlaw   paw   raw   saw   seesaw   straw   thaw

Other words that rhyme with *score*
corridor   dinosaur   door
drawer   floor   for   four
indoor   meteor   nor   or
outdoor   pour   war
your

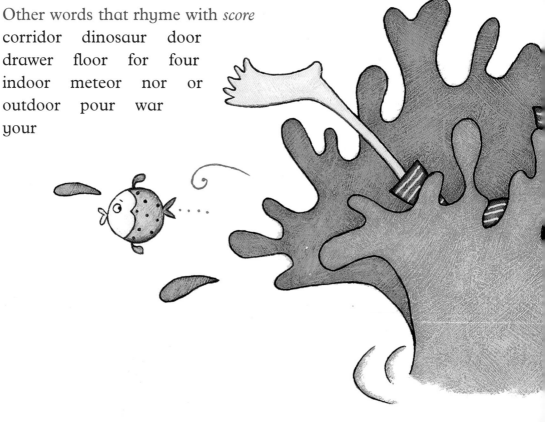

shirt
rhyming sound -irt

dirt   flirt   skirt   squirt

-irt rhymes with *-urt*
blurt   curt   hurt   spurt

-irt also rhymes with *-ert*
advert   alert   Bert   concert   desert
dessert   expert   pert

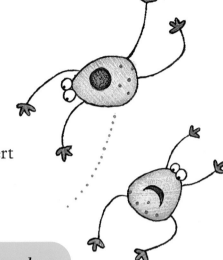

shop
rhyming sound -op

bop   chop   clop   cop   crop   drop   flip-flop   flop
hop   lollipop   lop   mop   plop   pop   prop   shop
slop   stop   top

Another word that rhymes
with *shop* is
swap

When the giant dived in the lake
There was an enormous plop,
And water flew up everywhere
'Cause he did a belly-flop.

a
b
c
d
e
f
g
h
i
j
k
l
m
n
o
p
q
r
s
t
u
v
w
x
y
z

smile   *rhyming sound -ile*

agile   awhile   crocodile   file   fragile
hostile   mile   missile   mobile   pile   profile
reptile   stile   tile   vile   while

Other words that rhyme with *smile*
aisle   dial   I'll   isle   style   trial

"I'll dine in style," said the crocodile,
Giving a smile,
As he sharpened his teeth with a file.

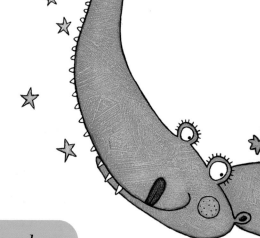

snow   *rhyming sound -ow*

arrow   below   blow   bow   burrow   crow   elbow   flow
glow   grow   hedgerow   know   low   marrow   meadow   mow
pillow   rainbow   row   scarecrow   shadow   shallow   show
slow   sorrow   sow   stow   throw   tomorrow   tow   window

-ow rhymes with *-o*
ago   armadillo   buffalo   commando   disco   domino   echo
go   halo   hello   hero   hippo   logo   macho   mosquito   no
patio   photo   piano   potato   radio   rodeo   so   solo   stereo
studio   tornado   UFO   video   volcano   yo-yo   zero

-ow also rhymes with *-oe*
doe   foe   hoe   Joe   mistletoe   oboe   toe   woe

Other words that rhyme with *snow*
although   dough   owe   sew   though

song

rhyming sound -ong

along   belong   bong   ding-dong
dong   gong   long   oblong   pong
prong   sarong   strong   throng
tong   wrong

spade

rhyming sound -ade

arcade   barricade   blade   decade   evade   fade
grade   invade   jade   lemonade   made
marmalade   parade   persuade   shade
trade   wade

-ade rhymes with *-aid*

afraid   aid   braid   laid   maid   mermaid   paid
raid   staid

-ade also rhymes with *-ayed*

arrayed   betrayed   decayed   delayed   frayed   played
prayed   sprayed   stayed   strayed   swayed   X-rayed

Other words that rhyme with *spade*
neighed   obeyed   preyed   suede   surveyed   weighed

Jade shook the bottle of lemonade,
Then she opened it and we all got sprayed.

speak — *rhyming sound -eak*

beak bleak creak freak leak peak sneak
squeak streak weak

-eak rhymes with *-eek*
cheek creek Greek leek meek peek reek seek
sleek week

-eak also rhymes with *-ique*
antique boutique clique technique unique

Another word that rhymes with *speak* is
shriek

Two ghosts are playing hide-and-shriek.
They've been seeking each other since last week.

sport   *rhyming sound -ort*

airport   export   fort   import   passport   port   report
resort   short   snort   sort   support   transport

> Sean Short bought some shorts,
> The shorts were shorter than
> Sean Short thought.
> Sean Short's short shorts were so short
> Sean Short thought, "Sean you ought
> Not to have bought shorts so short."

-ort rhymes with *-aught*
caught   distraught   fraught   onslaught   taught

-ort also rhymes with *-ought*
bought   brought   fought   nought   ought   sought
thought

-ort words rhyme with some *-art* words
quart   thwart   wart

Other words that rhyme with *sport*
astronaut   court   juggernaut   taut

stamp   *rhyming sound -amp*

amp   camp   champ   clamp   cramp
damp   lamp   ramp   scamp   tramp

storm   *rhyming sound -orm*

dorm   form   norm   perform   uniform

-orm words rhyme with some *-arm* words
swarm   warm

sun
rhyming sound -un

begun   bun   fun   gun   nun   pun   run   shun   spun   stun

-un words also rhyme with some *-one* words
done   none   one   someone

-un words also rhyme with some *-on* words
son   ton   won

A rabbit raced a turtle.
The turtle easily won.
The rabbit came in second,
A little hot cross bun.

Anon

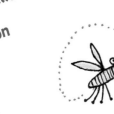

swim
rhyming sound -im

brim   dim   grim   him   Jim   Kim   prim   rim   skim   slim
Tim   trim   whim

Other words that rhyme with *swim*
gym   hymn   limb   pseudonym   synonym

a b c d e f g h i j k l m n o p q r s t u v w x y z

Tt

table
rhyming sound -able

able   cable   fable   stable   timetable

Another word that rhymes with *table* is
label

tail
rhyming sound -ail

ail bail detail fail frail hail jail mail nail pail
quail rail sail snail trail wail

-ail rhymes with *-ale*
ale bale dale exhale female gale impale inhale
male nightingale pale sale scale stale tale telltale
whale

A whale in a veil getting married in a gale.

Another word that rhymes with *tail* is
veil

talk

rhyming sound -alk

chalk   stalk   walk

-alk rhymes with *-ork*
cork   fork   pork   stork

-alk also rhymes with *-awk*
gawk   hawk   squawk   tomahawk

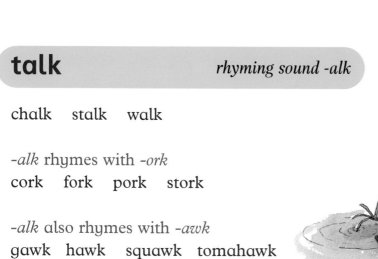

a
b
c
d
e
f
g
h
i
j
k
l
m
n
o
p
q
r
s
t
u
v
w
x
y
z

tent

rhyming sound -ent

accident   ascent   bent   cement   cent   compliment   consent
content   dent   descent   dissent   event   experiment   fragment
frequent   invent   lent   ornament   present   prevent   recent
relent   rent   resent   scent   sent   spent   torment   vent
went

Other words that rhyme with *tent*
leant   meant

We could not get rid of the scent
That a cow had left outside the tent!

tickle
rhyming sound -ickle

fickle   pickle   prickle   sickle   trickle

Another word that rhymes with *tickle* is
icicle

Don't tickle a thistle or you'll get in a pickle,
For thistles are prickly and thistles'll prickle.

tie

a
b
c
d
e
f
g
h
i
j
k
l
m
n
o
p
q
r
s
t
u
v
w
x
y
z

die   lie   pie   untie

-ie rhymes with *-y*
ally   butterfly   by   cry   deny   dry   fly   fry   horrify
July   lay-by   lullaby   magnify   multiply   my   mystify
nearby   petrify   pigsty   pry   rely   reply   satisfy   shy   sky
sly   spy   sty   supply   terrify   try   why   wry

-ie also rhymes with *-igh*
high   sigh   thigh

Other words that rhyme with *tie*
alibi   buy   bye   dye   eye   goodbye   I   guy

Georgie Porgie shouted "Hi!"
To a girl as she passed by.
"Give me a kiss. Don't be shy."
"Give you a kiss! I'd rather die."

time
rhyming sound -ime

chime   crime   grime   lime   mime   pantomine
prime   slime

Other words that rhyme with *time*
climb   enzyme   I'm   rhyme   thyme

tower
rhyming sound -ower

cauliflower   cower   flower   glower   power   shower

Some *-our* words rhyme with *tower*
devour   flour   hour   our   scour   sour

town
rhyming sound -own

brown   clown   crown   down   drown   frown   gown

Another word that rhymes with *town* is
noun

toy
rhyming sound -oy

ahoy   alloy   annoy   boy   buoy   convoy   corduroy
cowboy   coy   destroy   employ   enjoy   joy   ploy   Roy

tree
rhyming sound -ee

agree   bee   chimpanzee   coffee   degree   disagree   fee
flee   free   glee   guarantee   jamboree   jubilee   knee
marquee   pedigree   referee   refugee   see   settee   spree
tee   three   toffee   wee

-ee rhymes with *-ea*
flea   pea   plea   sea   tea

Other words that rhyme with *tree*
be   chimney   donkey   genie   grafitti
he   honey   key   macaroni   me   money
monkey   pixie   quay   recipe   she   ski
valley   we

trunk

rhyming sound -unk

bunk   chipmunk   chunk   clunk   drunk   dunk   hunk   junk
punk   shrunk   skunk   slunk   stunk   sunk

Another word that rhymes with *trunk* is
monk

"After the skunk slunk over my bunk,
it stunk!" said the monk.

Uu

under   *rhyming sound -under*

blunder   plunder   thunder

Another word that rhymes with *under* is
wonder

The pirates made a dreadful blunder
By trying to hide all their plunder
Beneath a tree during the thunder.
Now they're lying six feet under!

up   *rhyming sound -up*

buttercup   cup   hiccup   pickup   pup   sup

loot

114

urn
rhyming sound -urn

burn   churn   return   spurn   turn

-urn rhymes with *-earn*
earn   learn   yearn

-urn also rhymes with *-ern*
concern   fern   stern

us
rhyming sound -us

bonus   bus   cactus   circus   crocus   genius   hippopotamus
minus   octopus   plus   pus   radius   thus   virus   walrus

-us rhymes with *-uss*
discuss   fuss

-us also rhymes with *-ous*
anxious   callous   courageous   curious   dubious   enormous
envious   fabulous   famous   furious   glorious   gorgeous
hideous   hilarious   horrendous   ingenious   jealous   ludicrous
marvellous   mischievous   monstrous   mysterious   nervous
obvious   precious   raucous   ravenous   serious
tremendous   various   wondrous

The driver caused an awful fuss
When we tried to board the bus
With our hippopotamus.

use
rhyming sound -use

abuse   accuse   amuse   confuse   enthuse   excuse   fuse
muse   refuse   ruse

-use also rhymes with *-ews*
chews   news   screws   stews

-use also rhymes with *-ues*
blues   clues   hues   queues

-use also rhymes with *-ooze*
booze   ooze   snooze

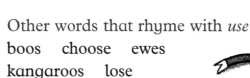

Other words that rhyme with *use*
boos   choose   ewes
kangaroos   lose
tattoos   views   whose   zoos

Gnus who choose to read the news
Share their views in queues in zoos.

Vv

van
rhyming sound -an

an ban began bran can caravan catamaran clan
deadpan fan flan gran Japan man marzipan nan
orang-utan pan plan ran scan span Stan tan than

A young man who came from Japan
Taught his orang-utan to cancan.
When I asked if he can,
The young man from Japan
Said, "Can he cancan? Yes, he can!"

vest   *rhyming sound -est*

arrest bequest best chest conquest contest
crest detest digest guest infest invest jest
lest nest pest protest quest request rest
suggest test west zest

-est rhymes with *-essed*
addressed blessed caressed
confessed depressed digressed
distressed dressed expressed
guessed impressed
messed obsessed
possessed
pressed
progressed
stressed

Ww

wall

rhyming sound -all

all ball call fall football hall mall pall small
squall stall tall

-all rhymes with *-awl*
bawl brawl crawl drawl
scrawl shawl sprawl
trawl

-all also rhymes with *-aul*
caterwaul haul maul
Paul

There was a young fellow called Paul
Who went to a fancy dress ball.
But he made a mistake
'Cause he went as a cake
And a dog ate him up in the hall.

a
b
c
d
e
f
g
h
i
j
k
l
m
n
o
p
q
r
s
t
u
w
x
y
z

weed

rhyming sound -eed

agreed   bleed   breed   creed   deed   exceed   freed
greed   guaranteed   heed   indeed   need   proceed
reed   refereed   seed   speed   steed   succeed   tweed

-eed words rhyme with some *-ead* words
bead   knead   lead   plead   read

-eed words rhyme with some *-ede* words
centipede   concede   millipede   stampede   swede

well

rhyming sound -ell

bell   cell   dwell   farewell   fell   hell   quell   sell
shell   smell   spell   swell   tell   unwell   yell

Other words that rhyme with *well*
caramel   carousel   excel   gel   hotel
lapel   motel   parallel
propel   rebel

Spinning round on the carousel
Sound the horn and ring the bell.
Feel the fairground's magic spell
Spinning round on the carousel.

a
b
c
d
e
f
g
h
i
j
k
l
m
n
o
p
q
r
s
t
u
v
w
x
y
z

wheel   *rhyming sound -eel*

eel feel heel keel kneel peel reel steel

-eel rhymes with *-eal*
appeal conceal deal heal ideal meal ordeal peal
real reveal seal squeal steal veal zeal

win   *rhyming sound -in*

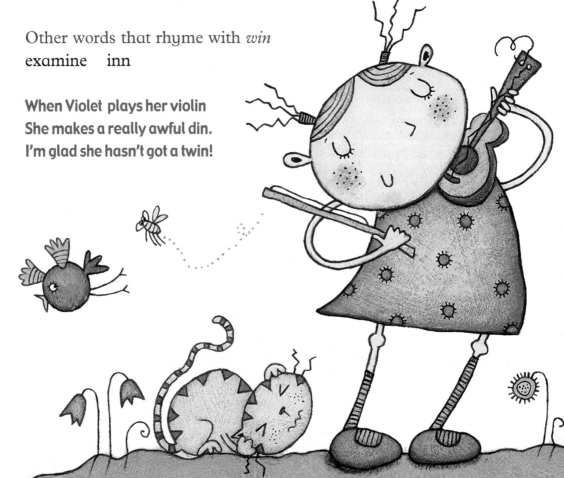

begin bin cabin chin coffin din dolphin fin goblin
gremlin grin in javelin kin margin muffin origin
penguin pin puffin pumpkin robin ruin satin sequin
shin sin skin spin thin tin twin
violin vitamin within

Other words that rhyme with *win*
examine inn

When Violet plays her violin
She makes a really awful din.
I'm glad she hasn't got a twin!

wise

advertise   advise   apologise   arise   clockwise   disguise
exercise   guise   likewise   organise   prise   revise   rise
sunrise   surprise

-ise rhymes with *-ies*
cries   dies   dries   flies   fries   horrifies   lies   lullabies
petrifies   pies   replies   skies   spies   terrifies   ties   tries

-ise also rhymes with *-ize*
capsize   hypnotize   idolise   prize
realize   recognize   size

Other words that rhyme with *wise*
buys   eyes   highs   sighs   thighs

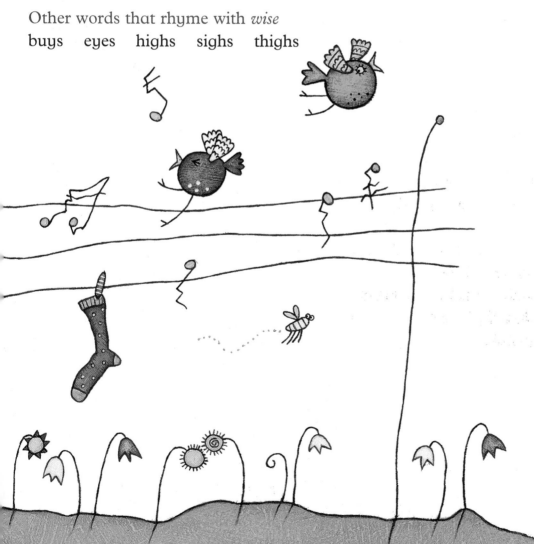

Xx

X-ray
rhyming sound -ay

alleyway anyway away bay betray birthday bray clay day decay delay display essay fray hay holiday hooray hurray lay may midday Monday (etc) motorway OK pay pray railway ray say spray stay stowaway straightaway subway sway takeaway today tray way yesterday

-ay rhymes with *-eigh*
neigh sleigh weigh

-ay also rhymes with *-ey*
disobey grey hey obey prey survey they

Other words that rhyme with *X-ray*
ballet bret bouquet buffet cafe chalet croquet duvet fiancé(e) paté ricochet sachet

When Auntie Fay began to neigh
And spend the day just eating hay,
My uncle said, "I cannot say
Why she's behaving in this way.
I'd better put her in the stable
In the stall next to your Auntie Mabel."

a
b
c
d
e
f
g
h
i
j
k
l
m
n
o
p
q
r
s
t
u
v
w
x
y
z

a
b
c
d
e
f
g
h
i
j
k
l
m
n
o
p
q
r
s
t
u
v
w
x
y
z

Yy

yard

rhyming sound -ard

bard   bombard   card   discard   hard
lard   leotard   postcard   regard   shard

-ard rhymes with *-arred*
barred   charred   jarred   marred
scarred   sparred   starred   tarred

Another word that rhymes with *yard* is
guard

yellow

rhyming sound -ellow

bellow   fellow   mellow

Other words that rhyme with *yellow*
cello   hello

I was practising playing the cello,
When I heard someone give a loud bellow,
"For goodness sake
You make my ears ache.
Please stop it. There's a good fellow!"

a
b
c
d
e
f
g
h
i
j
k
l
m
n
o
p
q
r
s
t
u
v
w
x
y
z

Zz

zip
rhyming sound -ip

blip championship chip clip dip drip equip fingertip
flip friendship gossip grip hardship hip kip leadership
lip microchip nip paperclip pip quip rip ship sip
skip slip snip strip tip trip tulip whip

zoo
rhyming sound -oo

a-choo bamboo boo coo cuckoo hullaballoo igloo
kangaroo loo moo shampoo shoo tattoo too voodoo
woo yoo-hoo

-oo rhymes with *-ew*
askew blew brew chew corkscrew crew dew drew
few flew grew interview knew mew nephew new
pew phew screw shrew sinew skew slew threw view

-oo also rhymes with *-ue*
argue avenue barbecue blue clue continue cue due
flue fondue glue hue queue revue rue statue subdue
sue tissue true value venue

Other words that rhyme with *zoo*
canoe   do   ewe   flu   gnu   guru
Hindu   kung fu   menu   Peru
rendezvous   shoe   tai-kwando
through   to   tutu
two   you

There was an old man from Peru
Who dreamed he was eating his shoe
He woke in the night
In a terrible fright
And found it was perfectly true.

Anon

a
b
c
d
e
f
g
h
i
j
k
l
m
n
o
p
q
r
s
t
u
v
w
x
y
z

Write your own poetry

Limericks

A limerick is a five line verse which follows a set pattern. It was first made famous by the poet Edward Lear (1812-88). You can find examples of limericks on pages 58 (**There was once a boy called Bill**), 117 (**A young man who came from Japan**) and 129 (**There was an old man from Peru**).

In a limerick
> lines 1 and 2 are longer lines that end with a rhyme
> lines 3 and 4 are shorter lines that end with a rhyme
> line 5 is a longer line that rhymes with lines 1 and 2

Can you complete these limericks?

> **There was a young schoolboy called Flynn**
> **Who sat on a drawing pin**
> **He leapt up in the air...**

You can find words with the rhyming sound *-in* listed under the entry for **win** on page 122 and words with the rhyming sound *-air* under the entry for **air** on page 8.

> **A daring young girl from Dundee...**

You can find words with the rhyming sound *-ee* listed under the entry for **tree** on page 112.

> **A wizard's apprentice called Matt...**

You can find words with the rhyming sound *-at* listed under the entry for **hat** on page 49.

Now see if you can make up a limerick on your own. Try to think of a funny punchline to end it.

Nonsense nursery rhymes

Nonsense nursery rhymes are modern versions of traditional nursery rhymes. For example:

Mary had a little cow.
She fed it safety pins
And every time she milked the cow
The milk came out in tins.

Here are the first lines of some nonsense nursery rhymes.
Can you complete them?

‣ Mary had a little cat.
   She dressed it in a skirt...

‣ Little Miss Kettle
   Sat on a nettle...

‣ Humpty Dumpty sat on the sofa
   Watching cartoons on TV.

‣ Billy, my brother and I fell out
   And what do you think it was all about?

‣ Little Tom Tarpet sat on the carpet
   Licking a big ice cream...

‣ Dr Lester went to Chester...

‣ Little Bo-Peep can't get to sleep...

‣ Monday's child has a goofy grin...

131

Counting rhymes

A counting rhyme is a rhyme which includes counting.
Some rhymes count up to ten, others count backwards from 10
down to 1.

Can you complete these counting rhymes?

One, two

One, two
A bath full of glue

Three, four....

Ten Naughty Dragons

Ten naughty dragons blowing smoke-rings in a line,
One set himself on fire then there were nine.

Nine naughty dragons....

Animal Counting Rhyme

One for the goat in a winter coat.
Two for the ants in striped underpants,
Three for the...

Ten Young Children

Ten young children
 Playing in the park.
The first one said,
 "Pretend I'm a shark."
The second one said,
 "I'm a dinosaur."
The third one said...

Rhyming riddles

The poems on this page are rhyming riddles. Can you solve them?

1

I can spin. I can roll. I can fly through the air.
I go where you hit me. Then I lie waiting there.
    I am usually round – sometimes big, sometimes small.
      I can make my way over or back from a wall.

2

    My first is in ghoul and also in charm.
   My second is in magic and twice in alarm.
 My third is in cauldron but isn't in fire.
My fourth is in gremlin but not in vampire.
My fifth is in skeleton and in bones.
My sixth is in werewolf but isn't in groans.
My seventh is in spell but not in broomstick.
My eighth's found in treat, but not found in trick.
My ninth is in phantom but isn't in fear.
My whole is the scariest night of the year.

3

Hold it steady in your hand,
Then you will see another land,
Where right is left, and left is right,
And no sound stirs by day or night;
When you look in, yourself you'll see,
Yet in that place you cannot be.

1. ball 2. Halloween 3. mirror

Here is a riddle about an animal with the rhyming words missing. Can you work out what the words are and what the animal is?

> I scratch the leaves that have fallen ____
> I am hard to see as my spines are ____
> I use the strong claws upon my ___
> To search for insects and slugs to ___ .
> Soon I'll curl in a ball in my ____
> And go to sleep for my winter ____

Make up a rhyming riddle of you own. Either choose a subject yourself or write a riddle about an animal or an object, such as a pen, a book or a bicycle.

Epitaphs

An epitaph is a verse written about a person or animal who has died. It is often put on their gravestone. Here are some examples:

> Here lies the body
> Of Percy Thistle
> A ref who's blown
> His final whistle.

> Here lies a teacher Mr Lee
> Who said, "You'll be the death of me"!
> And sitting at his desk one day
> He gave a sigh and passed away.

> In loving memory of Rover
> Who ran out in the road
> And got run over.

Answers: down brown feet eat nest rest (a hedgehog)

In memory of Charlotte Cul-de-sac,
A loyal and trusted friend
Who finally lived up to her name
And came to a dead end.

Can you complete these epitaphs?

▸ Here lie the remains of Auntie Vi
Who strapped on wings and tried to fly...

▸ In memory of Billy Green
Who took off in a time machine...

▸ Here lies what's left of Mr Bloor...

▸ Here lies a careless boy called Jake...

▸ In memory of fearless Fred...

▸ In memory of little Red Riding Hood...

Can you write some epitaphs of your own?

You could write about a person or an animal – either real or imaginary. For example, you could write about a nursery rhyme character, such as Old King Cole, an imaginary creature, such as Desmond Dinosaur, or a person with an unusual name, such as Candy Bar.

Rapping

Rapping is a popular type of rhyming poetry. A rap is a poem with plenty of rhyming and a very strong rhythm, which is often written to be performed.

Can you add some verses to this rap about people and their names?

Clap your hands, tap your feet,
Get the rhythm, get the beat.

My name's Grace. I am just ace.
I have got a smile on my face.

Clap your hands, tap your feet,
Get the rhythm, get the beat.

My name's Nasreen. I'm lean and mean.
I'm a star of the disco scene.

Clap your hands, tap your feet,
Get the rhythm, get the beat...

Can you write a fairground rap?
Here are two lines that you can use to get started:

C'mon everybody, let's go to the fair,
There's plenty of things for us to do there...

You can write a rap about any topic.
Choose your own subject and write a rap about it.
You could use these two lines to start your rap:

Come on everybody, let's hear you clap
We're going to do the ... rap.

Rhyming couplets

One of the ways poets use rhymes is to write rhyming couplets.
A rhyming couplet is a pair of lines that rhyme.

Example:

> We like riding on the double-decker bus,
> Up on the top-deck, that's the place for us!

Can you add some rhyming couplets to this list poem?

In my magic box

> In my magic box, I will put
>
> The twang of a guitar
> The silver lining of a star
>
> The juicy ripeness of a peach
> The sunlight shining on a beach...

Here is cautionary rhyme, written in couplets:

Warning: Too Much TV Can Damage Your Health

> This is the tale of Millie Mee
> Who day and night would watch TV.
> Now both her eyeballs have turned square,
> An aerial's growing in her hair.
> All she can do is watch TV
> For Millie's glued to the settee.
> So switch off now. Don't hesitate.
> Make sure you don't share Millie's fate.

Can you write some more couplets to complete these cautionary rhymes?

This is the tale of Samuel Sprocket
Who set off in his homemade rocket...

This is the tale of Betty Blair
Who never ever washed her hair...

A cheeky boy called Robert Rung
Was always sticking out his tongue..

Write a cautionary tale of your own, for example about someone who is always picking his nose or who is always boasting or about someone who does something silly. Write it in rhyming couplets.

Chants

Many chants, like this traditional one, are written in rhyming couplets:

Sam, Sam, the Dirty Old Man

Sam, Sam, the dirty old man,
Washed his face in a frying pan.
He combed his hair with a donkey's tail
And scratched his belly with his big toenail.

Teacher, Teacher

Teacher, teacher, please come quick
Jennifer Brown's been terribly sick.

Can you complete these 'Teacher, teacher' chants?

Teacher, teacher, what should I do?...

Teacher, teacher, come and have a look...

Teacher, teacher, look over there...

Teacher, teacher, help me please...

I Know a Man...

I know a man who wears smelly socks.
I know a man who thinks he's a fox.

Can you complete these 'I know a man' chants?

I know a man with toes on his head...

I know a man whose nose is square...

I know a man who lives in a drain...

I know a man who's the size of a flea...

Homophones

A homophone is one of a group of words which sound the same but have a different meaning or spelling. For example, hare and hair are homophones.

Can you find the homophones in these rhymes?

Bare Bear hasn't any hair.
That's why Bare Bear is bare.

Nobody asked her to dance at all,
So she had a good bawl at the ball.

"No, I don't know what to do,"
I said to the man in the queue.
"So I'll take my cue from you."

139

A gnu who was new to the zoo
Asked another gnu what he should do.
The other gnu said,
Shaking his head,
"If I knew, I'd tell you, I'm new too!"

Rose grows rows of roses.
Each rose Rose grows grows in a row.

Now use this dictionary to find homophones for these words:

beach   board   great   need   pale   pane
pear   read   right   road   sell   sew   sore   stair

Which of the above words has more than one other homophone?

Rhyme patterns

Many poems have four-line verses. A four-line verse is called a quatrain.
Quatrains can have a number of different rhyming patterns.

Pattern 1

In this verse the first and second lines rhyme and the third and fourth
lines rhyme.

As I was going out one day
My head fell off and rolled away.
But when I saw that it was gone,
I picked it up and put it on.

Can you complete the second verse of the poem?

And when I got into the ....
A fellow cried, "Look at your ....!"
I looked at them and sadly .....
"I've left them both asleep in ....!"

140

Pattern 2

This poem has verses in which the second line rhymes with the fourth line.

> We are the gremlins.
>   We're up to no good.
>   We do things we shouldn't,
>   Not things that we should.

> We get up to mischief
>   Of every sort.
> But we're cunning and clever,
> We never get caught.

Can you complete the next verse of the poem?

> We are the gremlins.
> We disconnect wires...

Can you add some more verses in the same pattern describing other things that the gremlins do?

Pattern 3

In this verse the first line rhymes with the third line and the second line rhymes with the fourth line.

> When the night is as cold as stone,
> When lightning severs the sky,
> When your blood is chilled to the bone,
> That's the hour when the witches fly.

Can you complete this verse about a mad magician using the same rhyme pattern?

> In his dark cave the mad magician dwells...

Pattern 4

Sometimes poets write lines in which there is a rhyme within the line. For example:

When Aunty Joan became a phone...

This is known as internal rhyme.

In the following verse the second line rhymes with the fourth line and there are internal rhymes in the first and third lines:

Elastic Jones had rubber bones.
He could bounce up and down like a ball.
When he was six, one of his tricks
Was jumping a ten-foot wall.

Can you complete this verse using the same rhyme pattern:

Ferdinand Fry boasted, "I can fly!"...

Now try to write a poem about a pirate called Peg-Leg Poll in four-line verses, using one of these rhyming patterns.

Index of rhyming sounds

-*ab* see **crab**
-*able* see **table**
-*ace* see **face**
-*aced* see **paste**
-*ack* see **back**
-*acked* see **act**
-*act* see **act**
-*ad* see **dad**
-*ade* see **spade**
-*ag* see **flag**
-*age* see **page**
-*aid* see **spade**
-*aight* see **gate**
-*ail* see **tail**
-*aim* see **name**
-*ain* see **rain**
-*aint* see **paint**
-*air* see **air**
-*aire* see **air**
-*airy* see **hairy**
-*aist* see **paste**
-*ait* see **gate**
-*ake* see **lake**
-*ale* see **tail**
-*alk* see **talk**
-*all* see **wall**
-*alm* see **arm**
-*am* see **jam**
-*ame* see **name**
-*amp* see **stamp**
-*an* see **van**
-*ance* see **dance**
-*and* see **hand**
-*ane* see **rain**

-*ang* see **bang**
-*ank* see **bank**
-*anned* see **hand**
-*ant* see **ant**
-*ap* see **map**
-*ape* see **grape**
-*ar* see **car**
-*ard* see **yard**
-*are* see **air**
-*ark* see **dark**
-*arm* (as in harm) see **arm**
-*arm* (as in warm) see **storm**
-*arred* see **yard**
-*art* (as in start) see **cart**
-*art* (as in wart) see **sport**
-*ary* see **hairy**
-*ase* see **face**
-*ash* see **crash**
-*ask* see **ask**
-*ass* see **glass**
-*ast* see **last**
-*aste* see **paste**
-*at* see **hat**
-*atch* see **catch**
-*ate* see **gate**
-*aught* see **sport**
-*aul* see **wall**
-*ave* see **cave**
-*aw* see **score**
-*awk* see **talk**
-*awl* see **wall**

-*awn* see **corn**
-*ay* see **X-ray**
-*ayed* see **spade**
-*ayer* see **air**

-*ea* see **tree**
-*each* see **beach**
-*ead* (as in head) see **red**
-*ead* (as in bead) see **weed**
-*eak* (as in beak) see **speak**
-*eak* (as in break) see **cake**
-*eal* see **wheel**
-*eam* see **dream**
-*ean* see **queen**
-*eap* see **keep**
-*ear* (as in fear) see **ear**
-*ear* (as in bear) see **air**
-*earn* see **urn**
-*eas* see **freeze**
-*ease* see **freeze**
-*east* see **east**
-*eat* (as in heat) see **meat**
-*eat* (as in sweat) see **jet**
-*eck* see **neck**
-*ed* see **red**
-*ede* see **weed**
-*ee* see **tree**
-*eech* see **beach**

-*eed* see **weed**
-*eek* see **speak**
-*eel* see **wheel**
-*eem* see **dream**
-*een* see **queen**
-*eep* see **keep**
-*eer* see **ear**
-*ees* see **freeze**
-*eet* see **meat**
-*eeze* see **freeze**
-*eg* see **leg**
-*eigh* see **X-ray**
-*el* see **well**
-*elf* see **elf**
-*ell* see **well**
-*ellow* see **yellow**
-*elt* see **belt**
-*en* see **hen**
-*end* see **end**
-*ene* see **queen**
-*ent* see **tent**
-*ept* see **crept**
-*er* (as in her) see **fur**
-*erd* see **bird**
-*ere* (as in here) see **ear**
-*ere* (as in where) see **air**
-*ere* (as in were) see **fur**
-*ern* see **urn**
-*erry* see **merry**
-*ert* see **shirt**
-*ess* see **dress**

-essed see **vest**

-est see **vest**

-et see **jet**

-ete see **meat**

-ette see **jet**

-ettle see **nettle**

-ever see **ever**

-ew (as in chew)
see **zoo**

-ew (as in sew)
see **snow**

-ewed see **food**

-ewn (as in sewn)
see **bone**

-ews (as in sews)
see **nose**

-ews (as in news)
see **use**

-ey (as in key)
see **tree**

-ey (as in they)
see **X-ray**

-ic see **quick**

-ice (as in ice)
see **ice**

-ice (as in practice)
see **kiss**

-ich see **itch**

-ick see **quick**

-ickle see **tickle**

-icks see **mix**

-ics see **mix**

-id see **lid**

-iddle see **middle**

-ide see **ride**

-idge see **bridge**

-ie see **tie**

-ied see **ride**

-ier see **ear**

-ies see **wise**

-iews (as in views)
see **use**

-ig see **big**

-igh see **tie**

-ighs see **wise**

-ight see **light**

-ign see **nine**

-ike see **bike**

-il see **ill**

-ile see **smile**

-ill see **ill**

-im see **swim**

-ime see **time**

-imp see **imp**

-in see **win**

-ind see **find**

-ine (as in
magazine)
see **queen**

-ine (as in fine)
see **nine**

-ing see **king**

-ink see **ink**

-inner see **dinner**

-int see **print**

-ip see **zip**

-ique see **speak**

-ir see **fur**

-ird see **bird**

-ire see **fire**

-irl see **girl**

-irr see **fur**

-irst see **first**

-irt see **shirt**

-ise (as in rise)
see **wise**

-ise (as in promise)
see **kiss**

-ise (as in paradise)
see **ice**

-ish see **fish**

-iss see **kiss**

-issed see **mist**

-ist see **mist**

-it see **hit**

-itch see **itch**

-ite see **light**

-ive see **five**

-iver see **river**

-ix see **mix**

-ize see **wise**

-o (as in slow)
see **snow**

-oad see **road**

-oak see **oak**

-oal see **hole**

-oap see **rope**

-oar see **score**

-oard see **lord**

-oast see **post**

-oat see **coat**

-ob see **job**

-ock see **knock**

-ocks see **fox**

-ode see **road**

-oe see **snow**

-oes see **nose**

-og see **dog**

-ogue see **dog**

-oil see **oil**

-oke see **oak**

-old see **old**

-ole see **hole**

-oll see **hole**

-ome (as in come)
see **mum**

-on (as in son)
see **sun**

-ond see **pond**

-onder see **under**

-one (as in phone)
see **bone**

-one (as in one)
see **sun**

-oney see **honey**

-ong see **song**

-oo see **zoo**

-ood (as in food)
see **food**

-ood (as in blood)
see **mud**

-ood (as in wood)
see **hood**

-ooed see **food**

-ook see **cook**

-ool see **pool**

-ool (as in wool)
see **pull**

-oom see **room**

-oon see **moon**

-oop see **hoop**

-oot see **boot**

-oor see **score**

-ooze see **use**

-op see **shop**

-ope see **rope**

-or see **score**

-ord see **lord**

-ore see **score**

-ored see **lord**

-ork see **talk**

-orm see **storm**

-orn see **corn**

-ort see **sport**

-os (as in radios) see **nose**

-ose see **nose**

-oss see **boss**

-ost see **post**

-ot see **pot**

-ote see **coat**

-other see **brother**

-ouble see **bubble**

-ough (as in rough) see **puff**

-ough (as in plough) see **cow**

-ought see **sport**

-ould see **hood**

-ounce see **bounce**

-ound see **round**

-oup see **hoop**

-our (as in pour) see **score**

-our (as in hour) see **tower**

-ous see **us**

-ouse see **house**

-out see **out**

-ove see **love**

-ow (as in now) see **cow**

-ow (as in blow) see **snow**

-owed see **road**

-owel see **owl**

-ower see **tower**

-owl see **owl**

-own see **town**

-own (as in phone, groan) see **bone**

-owned (as in crowned) see **round**

-ows see **nose**

-ox see **fox**

-oy see **toy**

-oyal see **oil**

-oze see **nose**

-ub see **grub**

-ubble see **bubble**

-uck see **duck**

-ud see **mud**

-ude see **food**

-ue see **zoo**

-ued see **food**

-ues (as in clues) see **use**

-uff see **puff**

-ug see **jug**

-ul see **pull**

-ule see **pool**

-ull see **pull**

-um see **mum**

-umb see **mum**

-umble see **rumble**

-ume see **room**

-ump see **jump**

-un see **sun**

-unch see **lunch**

-under see **under**

-une see **moon**

-ung see **lung**

-unk see **trunk**

-unny see **honey**

-unt see **hunt**

-up see **up**

-ur see **fur**

-url see **girl**

-urn see **urn**

-urr see **fur**

-urt see **shirt**

-us see **us**

-use see **use**

-ush see **rush**

-uss see **us**

-ust see **dust**

-ut see **hut**

-ute see **boot**

-uy see **tie**

-y see **tie**

-ye see **tie**

-yme see **time**

Alphabetical index

before *98*
beg *67*
began *117*
begin *122*
beginner *29*
begun *105*
behave *20*
behind *36*
behold *82*
bell *120*
bellow *127*
bellows *80*
belong *101*
below *100*
belt *12*
Ben *49*
bend *33*
bent *108*
bequest *118*
beret *124*
berry *73*
Bert *99*
beside *92*
best *118*
bet *60*
betray *124*
betrayed *101*
between *89*
beware *8*
beyond *85*
bid *67*
big *12*
bike *12*
bill *58*
billionaire *8*
bin *122*
bind *36*
bird *12*
birthday *124*
biscuit *49*
bit *49*
bite *68*

bizarre *18*
black *13*
blackout *83*
blade *101*
blame *76*
blank *11*
blare *8*
blast *66*
bleach *11*
bleak *102*
bleat *72*
bled *91*
bleed *120*
bleep *63*
blend *33*
bless *30*
blessed *118*
blew *128*
blind *36*
blink *59*
blip *128*
bliss *65*
blob *61*
block *65*
blocks *41*
bloke *81*
blond *85*
blood *75*
bloom *95*
blot *87*
blow *100*
blown *14*
blows *80*
blue *128*
blues *116*
bluff *88*
blunder *114*
blunt *55*
blur *44*
blurred *12*
blurt *99*
blush *97*
boar *98*

board *69*
boast *86*
boat *20*
bob *61*
bog *29*
boil *81*
bold *82*
bombard *126*
bond *85*
bone *14*
bonfire *38*
bong *101*
bonus *115*
boo *128*
booed *40*
boo-hooed *40*
book *21*
bookcase *34*
bookshelf *33*
boom *95*
boomerang *10*
boos *116*
boot *15*
booze *116*
bop *99*
bore *98*
bored *69*
boring *64*
born *22*
borne *22*
boss *16*
bough *23*
bought *103*
bounce *16*
bound *96*
bouquet *124*
bout *83*
boutique *102*
bow *23*

bow *100*
bowel *83*
bowl *50*
bowled *82*
bows *80*
bow-wow *23*
box *41*
brace *34*
braced *85*
bracelet *60*
brag *39*
braid *101*
brain *90*
brake *66*
bran *117*
brand *48*
brass *46*
brat *49*
brave *20*
brawl *119*
bray *124*
bread *91*
break *66*
bred *91*
breed *120*
breeze *42*
brew *128*
brewed *40*
brick *89*
bricks *74*
bride *92*
bridegroom *95*
bridge *16*
brill *58*
brim *105*
brine *79*
bring *64*
brink *59*
broad *69*
broil *81*
broke *81*
brood *40*

brook *21*
broom *95*
broomsticks *74*
brother *17*
brought *103*
brow *23*
brown *112*
browned *96*
brunch *70*
brush *97*
brute *15*
bubble *17*
buccaneer *32*
buck *30*
bucket *60*
bud *75*
buff *88*
buffalo *100*
buffet *124*
bug *61*
bull *88*
bulldoze *80*
bumble *96*
bump *61*
bun *105*
bunch *70*
bung *70*
bungalows *80*
bunk *113*
bunny *52*
buoy *112*
burn *115*
burrow *100*
burrowed *94*
burst *39*
bury *73*
bus *115*
bust *30*
but *55*

buttercup *114*
butterfly *110*
buy *110*
buys *123*
by *110*
bye *110*
bypass *46*
byte *68*

C
cab *23*
cabin *122*
cable *106*
cactus *115*
cafe *124*
cage *84*
cajoled *82*
cake *66*
calculate *45*
call *119*
callous *115*
calm *10*
came *76*
camp *104*
can *117*
canary *48*
candyfloss *16*
cane *90*
canned *48*
cannot *87*
canoe *129*
canteen *89*
cap *71*
cape *46*
capsize *123*
capsule *86*
car *18*
caramel *120*
caravan *117*
card *126*

cardboard 69
care 8
career 32
careful 88
caressed 118
carnivore 98
carousel 120
carpet 60
cart 19
cartoon 75
case 34
cash 24
cashier 32
cask 10
casserole 50
cassette 60
cast 66
cat 49
catalogue 29
catamaran 117
catch 19
caterwaul 119
caught 103
cauliflower 111
cavalier 32
cave 20
caviar 18
caw 98
ceased 33
ceiling 64
celebrate 45
cell 120
cello 127
celt 12
cement 108
cent 108
centipede 120
chain 90

chair 8
chalet 124
chalk 107
champ 104
championship 128
chance 27
chap 71
charm 10
charred 126
chart 19
chase 34
chased 85
chat 49
cheap 63
cheat 72
check 78
cheek 102
cheep 63
cheer 32
cheerful 88
cheese 42
cheque 78
cherry 73
chess 30
chest 118
chestnut 55
chew 128
chewed 40
chews 116
chick 89
chicks 74
childhood 54
chill 58
chime 111
chimney 112
chimneys 42
chimp 59
chimpanzee 112
chimpanzees 42
chin 122

chink 59
chip 128
chipmunk 113
choir 38
choke 81
choose 116
chop 99
chord 69
chore 98
chose 80
chuck 30
chug 61
chum 75
chunk 113
churn 115
chute 15
cigar 18
circuit 49
circus 115
clad 27
claim 76
clamp 104
clan 117
clang 10
clank 11
clap 71
clarinet 60
clash 24
class 46
classed 66
claw 98
clay 124
clean 89
clear 32
clever 33
click 89
clicks 74
climb 111
cling 64
clink 59
clip 128
clique 102

cloak 81
clock 65
clocks 41
clockwise 123
clog 29
clone 14
clop 99
close 80
clot 87
clout 83
clown 112
clowned 96
club 47
cluck 30
clue 128
clues 116
clump 61
clung 70
clunk 113
coal 50
coast 86
coat 20
cob 61
code 94
coffee 112
coffin 122
coil 81
coke 81
cold 82
collide 92
combat 49
combine 79
come 75
comic 89
commando 100
commonplace 34
compact 8
compare 8
compete 72
complain 90

complaint 85
complete 72
compliment 108
conceal 122
concede 120
concentrate 45
concern 115
concert 99
concrete 72
cone 14
confess 30
confessed 118
confiscate 45
confuse 116
conquest 118
consent 108
console 50
consoled 82
contact 8
contain 90
content 108
contest 118
continue 128
contract 8
contrary 48
contrast 66
control 50
controlled 82
convoy 112
coo 128
cooed 40
cook 21
cool 86
coop 54
cop 99
cope 96
cord 69

corduroy 112
core 98
cork 107
corkscrew 128
corn 22
corridor 98
costume 95
cot 87
could 54
countryside 92
courageous 115
courgette 60
court 103
cow 23
cowboy 112
cower 111
cox 41
coy 112
crab 23
crack 13
cracked 8
crag 39
cram 60
cramp 104
crane 90
crank 11
crash 24
crate 45
crave 20
crawl 119
creak 102
cream 29
creased 33
create 45
creed 120
creek 102
creep 63
crept 26
cress 30

crest *118*
crew *128*
cricket *60*
cried *92*
cries *123*
crime *111*
crimp *59*
croak *81*
crock *65*
crocodile *100*
crocus *115*
crook *21*
croon *75*
crop *99*
croquet *124*
cross *16*
crow *100*
crowed *94*
crown *112*
crowned *96*
crows *80*
crude *40*
crumb *75*
crumble *96*
crunch *70*
crush *97*
crust *30*
cry *110*
cub *47*
cuckoo *128*
cud *75*
cue *128*
cuff *88*
culprit *49*
cup *114*
curious *115*
curl *46*
currant *10*
cursed *39*
curt *99*
cut *55*
cute *15*

cyclist *74*
Czeck *78*

D
dab *23*
dad *27*
daffodil *58*
dairy *48*
dale *106*
dam *60*
damp *104*
dance *27*
dandruff *88*
dank *11*
dare *8*
dark *28*
dart *19*
dash *24*
database *34*
date *45*
dawn *22*
day *124*
daydream *29*
dead *91*
deadpan *117*
deadwood *54*
deal *122*
dealt *12*
dear *32*
debate *45*
debt *60*
decade *101*
decay *124*
decayed *101*
deceased *33*
decide *92*
deck *78*
declare *8*
decorate *45*
deed *120*

deep *63*
deer *32*
defeat *72*
defend *33*
defied *92*
define *79*
degree *112*
degrees *42*
delay *124*
delayed *101*
delete *72*
delight *68*
deliver *93*
den *49*
denied *92*
dent *108*
deny *110*
depart *19*
depend *33*
depress *30*
depressed *118*
descend *33*
descendant *10*
descent *108*
desert *99*
design *79*
desire *38*
despair *8*
dessert *99*
destroy *112*
detach *19*
detail *106*
detest *118*
devote *20*
devour *111*
dew *128*
dial *100*
dice *56*
did *67*
diddle *73*
die *110*

died *92*
dies *123*
dig *12*
digest *118*
digressed *118*
dilute *15*
dim *105*
din *122*
dine *79*
dined *36*
ding *64*
ding-dong *101*
dinner *29*
dinosaur *98*
dip *128*
dire *38*
dirt *99*
disagree *112*
disappear *32*
discard *126*
disco *100*
discotheque *78*
discreet *72*
discuss *115*
disease *42*
disgrace *34*
disgraced *85*
disguise *123*
disgust *30*
dish *39*
dislike *12*
dismiss *65*
dismissed *74*
disobey *124*
display *124*
dispute *15*
dissent *108*
distract *8*
distraught *103*

distress *30*
distressed *118*
ditch *59*
dive *39*
divide *92*
divine *79*
dock *65*
docks *41*
doe *100*
dog *29*
dole *50*
dolphin *122*
domino *100*
dominoes *80*
done *105*
dong *101*
donkey *112*
donkeys *42*
doom *95*
door *98*
dope *96*
dorm *104*
dot *87*
dote *20*
double *17*
doubt *83*
doubtful *88*
dough *100*
doughnut *55*
dove *70*
down *112*
downed *96*
doze *80*
drab *23*
drag *39*
drain *90*
drake *66*
drank *11*
drape *46*
draw *98*
drawer *98*
drawl *119*

drawn *22*
dread *91*
dreadful *88*
dream *29*
dreg *67*
dress *30*
dressed *118*
drew *128*
dried *92*
dries *123*
driftwood *54*
drill *58*
drink *59*
drip *128*
drive *39*
drone *14*
drool *86*
droop *54*
drop *99*
drought *83*
drown *112*
drowned *96*
drug *61*
drum *75*
drunk *113*
dry *110*
dub *47*
dubious *115*
duck *30*
dud *75*
due *128*
duet *60*
duff *88*
dug *61*
dugout *83*
dumb *75*
dump *61*
dune *75*
dung *70*
dungarees *42*
dunk *113*
dust *30*

duvet *124*
dwell *120*
dwelt *12*
dye *110*
dyed *92*
dynamite *68*

E
each *11*
ear *32*
earl *46*
earn *115*
earshot *87*
earwig *12*
ease *42*
east *33*
eat *72*
echo *100*
educate *45*
eel *122*
egg *67*
eight *45*
elastic *89*
elbow *100*
elbows *80*
electric *89*
elegant *10*
elephant *10*
elf *33*
elope *96*
embark *28*
embrace *34*
embraced *85*
empire *38*
employ *112*
encore *98*
end *33*
engage *84*
engineer *32*
enjoy *112*
enormous
 115
enough *88*

enrage *84*
entertain *90*
enthuse *116*
entrance *27*
envelope *96*
envious *115*
enzyme *111*
episode *94*
equip *128*
erode *94*
escape *46*
essay *124*
estate *45*
estimate *45*
evade *101*
event *108*
ever *33*
ewe *129*
ewes *116*
exact *8*
exaggerate
 45
exam *60*
examine *122*
exceed *120*
excel *120*
except *26*
excess *30*
excite *68*
exclaim *76*
exclude *40*
excuse *116*
execute *15*
exercise *123*
exhale *106*
exit *49*
expand *48*
experiment
 108
expert *99*
explain *90*
explode *94*
explore *98*

explored *69*
export *103*
expose *80*
express *30*
expressed
 118
extend *33*
extract *8*
extreme *29*
eye *110*
eyebrow *23*
eyed *92*
eyes *123*

F
fab *23*
fable *106*
fabulous *115*
face *34*
faced *85*
fact *8*
fad *27*
fade *101*
fail *106*
faint *85*
fair *8*
fairy *48*
faithful *88*
fake *66*
fall *119*
falsehood *54*
fame *76*
famous *115*
fan *117*
fang *10*
fanned *48*
fantastic *89*
far *18*
fare *8*
farewell *120*
farm *10*
fascinate *45*
fast *66*

fat *49*
fate *45*
fawn *22*
fear *32*
fearful *88*
feast *33*
feat *72*
fed *91*
fee *112*
feed *120*
feel *122*
fees *42*
feet *72*
fell *120*
fellow *127*
felt *12*
female *106*
fen *49*
fern *115*
ferry *73*
fete *45*
fettle *78*
few *128*
fiancé(e)
 124
fickle *109*
fiddle *73*
fidget *60*
fig *12*
fight *68*
file *100*
fill *58*
fin *122*
find *36*
fine *79*
fined *36*
fingertip *128*
fir *44*
fire *38*
fireplace *34*
first *39*
fish *39*
fist *74*

fit *49*
five *39*
fix *74*
flab *23*
flag *39*
flair *8*
flake *66*
flame *76*
flan *117*
flap *71*
flapjack *13*
flash *24*
flask *10*
flat *49*
flaw *98*
flea *112*
fleas *42*
fleck *78*
fled *91*
flee *112*
flees *42*
fleet *72*
flew *128*
flick *89*
flicks *74*
flies *123*
fling *64*
flint *87*
flip *128*
flip-flop *99*
flirt *99*
flit *49*
float *20*
flock *65*
flocks *41*
flog *29*
flood *75*
floor *98*
flop *99*
floss *16*
flounce *16*
flour *111*
flow *100*

flowed *94*
flower *111*
flown *14*
flows *80*
flu *129*
flue *128*
fluff *88*
flume *95*
flung *70*
flush *97*
flute *15*
fly *110*
flyer *38*
foal *50*
foe *100*
foes *80*
fog *29*
foil *81*
fold *82*
folk *81*
fond *85*
fondue *128*
food *40*
fool *86*
football *119*
footprint *87*
for *98*
forbid *67*
ford *69*
forever *33*
forgave *20*
forget *60*
forgot *87*
fork *107*
forlorn *22*
form *104*
fort *103*
fortune *75*
fought *103*
foul *83*
found *96*
four *98*
fourteen *89*

fowl 83
fox 41
fragile 100
fragment 108
frail 106
frame 76
France 27
frank 11
frantic 89
fraught 103
fray 124
frayed 101
freak 102
free 112
freed 120
freeze 42
frequent 108
fret 60
friar 38
fridge 16
fried 92
friend 33
friendship 128
fries 123
fright 68
frill 58
frock 65
frocks 41
frog 29
frogspawn 22
front 55
frontier 32
frown 112
frowned 96
froze 80
fruit 15
frump 61
frustrate 45
fry 110
fryer 38

fuel 86
fulfil 58
full 88
fumble 96
fume 95
fun 105
funny 52
fur 44
furious 115
furl 46
fuse 116
fuss 115

G
gadget 60
gag 39
gain 90
gale 106
galore 98
game 76
gang 10
gap 71
gape 46
gargoyle 81
gash 24
gate 45
gave 20
gawk 107
gear 32
gel 120
gene 89
genie 112
genius 115
get 60
ghost 86
ghoul 86
gig 12
gill 58
gimmick 89
gimmicks 74
girl 46
glad 27
glance 27

gland 48
glare 8
glass 46
gleam 29
glean 89
glee 112
glen 49
glide 92
glint 87
glitch 59
gloat 20
globule 86
gloom 95
glorious 115
gloss 16
glove 70
glow 100
glowed 94
glower 111
glows 80
glue 128
glued 40
glug 61
glum 75
glut 55
gnash 24
gnat 49
gnaw 98
gnu 129
go 100
goad 94
goal 50
goat 20
gob 61
goblin 122
goes 80
gold 82
gondolier 32
gong 101
good 54
goodbye 110
goosebump 61

gore 98
gorgeous 115
gossip 128
got 87
gown 112
grab 23
grace 34
graced 85
graceful 88
grade 101
graffiti 112
grain 90
gram 60
gran 117
grand 48
grape 46
grass 46
grate 45
gratitude 40
grave 20
greased 33
great 45
greed 120
Greek 102
green 89
greet 72
Greg 67
gremlin 122
grew 128
grey 124
grid 67
griddle 73
grill 58
grim 105
grime 111
grin 122
grind 36
grip 128
grit 49
groan 14
grog 29
groom 95

grope 96
ground 96
group 54
grow 100
growl 83
grown 14
grows 80
grub 47
gruff 88
grumble 96
grunt 55
guarantee 112
guaranteed 120
guard 126
guess 30
guessed 118
guest 118
guffaw 98
guide 92
guise 123
guitar 18
gum 75
gun 105
guru 129
gush 97
gust 30
gut 55
guy 110
gym 105

H
ha 18
habit 49
habitat 49
hack 13
had 27
hag 39
ha-ha 18
hail 106
hair 8
hairy 48

hall 119
halo 100
ham 60
hand 48
handcuff 88
hang 10
happiness 30
hard 126
hardship 128
hare 8
hark 28
harm 10
harmful 88
harpoon 75
hash 24
haste 85
hat 49
hatch 19
hate 45
haul 119
hawk 107
hay 124
haystack 13
he 112
head 91
headache 66
heal 122
heap 63
hear 32
heard 12
heart 19
heat 72
heatwave 20
hedgerow 100
heed 120
heel 122
height 68
heirloom 95
hell 120
hello 100
hello 127
helmet 60

helpless 30
hen 49
her 44
herd 12
here 32
hero 100
herself 33
hey 124
hiccup 114
hid 67
hide 92
hideous 115
hideout 83
high 110
higher 38
highs 123
high-tech 78
hijacked 8
hike 12
hilarious 115
hill 58
him 105
himself 33
Hindu 129
hint 87
hip 128
hippo 100
hippopota-
  mus 115
hire 38
hiss 65
hissed 74
hit 49
hitch 59
hive 39
hoard 69
hob 61
hobnob 61
hoe 100
hoes 80
hog 29
hold 82
hole 50

holiday 124
honey 52
honeymoon
  75
honey 112
hood 54
hook 21
hoop 54
hooray 124
hoot 15
hop 99
hope 96
hopeful 88
horde 69
horn 22
horoscope
  96
horrendous
  115
horrified 92
horrifies 123
horrify 110
horseback
  13
hose 80
host 86
hostile 100
hot 87
hotel 120
hound 96
hour 111
house 54
how 23
however 33
howl 83
hub 47
hubbub 47
hue 128
hues 116
huff 88
hug 61
hullaballoo
  128

hum 75
humble 96
hump 61
humpbacked
  8
hunch 70
hung 70
hunk 113
hunt 55
hurl 46
hurray 124
hurt 99
hush 97
hut 55
hygiene 89
hymn 105
hypnotize
  123

I
I 110
ice 56
ice cream 29
icicle 109
I'd 92
ideal 122
idolize 123
igloo 128
ignite 68
ignore 98
ignored 69
ill 58
I'll 100
I'm 111
imp 59
impact 8
impale 106
import 103
impress 30
impressed
  118
in 122
include 40

increased 33
indeed 120
indoor 98
inept 26
infest 118
ingenious
  115
inhale 106
ink 59
inn 122
inner 29
inquire 38
inside 92
insist 74
inspire 38
instead 91
intend 33
intercept 26
internet 60
interview
  128
intrude 40
invade 101
invent 108
invest 118
investigate
  45
invite 68
irritate 45
isle 100
it 49
itch 59
itself 33
I've 39

J
jab 23
jack 13
jackdaw 98
jacket 60
jackpot 87
jade 101
jaguar 18

jail 106
jam 60
jamboree
  112
Jane 90
Japan 117
jar 18
jarred 126
javelin 122
jaw 98
jealous 115
Jean 89
jeep 63
jeer 32
jest 118
jet 60
jig 12
Jill 58
Jim 105
jive 39
job 61
Joe 100
jog 29
joke 81
jot 87
joy 112
joyful 88
jubilee 112
jug 61
juggernaut
  103
July 110
jumble 96
jump 61
June 75
junk 113
just 30
jut 55

K
kangaroo
  128

kangaroos
  116
Kate 45
kayak 13
kebab 23
keel 122
keen 89
keep 63
keg 67
Ken 49
kept 26
kettle 78
key 112
keyboard 69
keys 42
kick 89
kicks 74
kid 67
kidnap 71
kill 58
Kim 105
kin 122
kind 36
kindness 30
king 64
kink 59
kip 128
kiss 65
kissed 74
kit 49
kite 68
knack 13
knave 20
knead 120
knee 112
kneel 122
knees 42
knelt 12
knew 128
knight 68
knit 49
knob 61
knock 65

knockout 83
knocks 41
knot 87
know 100
known 14
knows 80
kung fu 129

L
lab 23
label 106
lace 34
laced 85
lack 13
lacked 8
lad 27
ladybird 12
lag 39
lagoon 75
laid 101
lair 8
lake 66
lamb 60
lame 76
lamp 104
lance 27
land 48
landmark 28
landscape 46
lane 90
lank 11
lap 71
lapel 120
lard 126
lark 28
lash 24
last 66
latch 19
late 45
launderette 60
law 98

lawn 22
lay 124
lay-by 110
lead 91
lead 120
leadership 128
leak 102
lean 89
leant 108
leap 63
leapt 26
learn 115
least 33
led 91
leek 102
leer 32
leg 67
lemonade 101
Len 49
lend 33
lent 108
leotard 126
leprechaun 22
less 30
lest 118
let 60
liar 38
lice 56
lick 89
licks 74
lid 67
lie 110
lied 92
lies 123
light 68
like 12
likewise 123
limb 105
lime 111
limerick 89

limousine 89
limp 59
line 79
lined 36
link 59
lint 87
lip 128
liquid 67
liquorice 65
list 74
lit 49
live 39
liver 93
load 94
loan 14
lob 61
lock 65
locks 41
log 29
logo 100
lollipop 99
lone 14
loneliness 30
long 101
loo 128
look 21
lookout 83
loom 95
loop 54
loot 15
lop 99
lope 96
lord 69
lose 116
loss 16
lot 87
louse 54
lout 83
love 70
low 100
loyal 81
luck 30

ludicrous 115
lug 61
lullabies 123
lullaby 110
lumberjack 13
lump 61
lunch 70
lung 70
lush 97

M
ma 18
mac 13
macaroni 112
macaroon 75
macho 100
mad 27
made 101
magazine 89
magnet 60
magnify 110
maid 101
mail 106
maim 76
main 90
make 66
male 106
mall 119
man 117
mane 90
maniac 13
manned 48
map 71
mare 8
margin 122
marigold 82
mark 28
marmalade 101

maroon 75
marquee 112
marred 126
marrow 100
marvellous 115
Mary 48
marzipan 117
mascot 87
mash 24
mask 10
mast 66
mat 49
match 19
matchsticks 74
mate 45
matrix 74
maul 119
may 124
me 112
meadow 100
meadows 80
meal 122
mean 89
meant 108
meat 72
meek 102
meet 72
Meg 67
megaphone 14
mellow 127
melt 12
men 49
mend 33
menu 129
meow 23
mere 32
mermaid 101

merry 73
mess 30
messed 118
met 60
metal 78
meteor 98
mew 128
mewed 40
mice 56
microchip 128
microscope 96
microwave 20
mid-air 8
midday 124
middle 73
midge 16
midnight 68
might 68
mile 100
mill 58
millionaire 8
millipede 120
mime 111
mind 36
mine 79
mined 36
miniscule 86
mink 59
mint 87
minus 115
minute 15
mischievous 115
mis-match 19
misplace 34
miss 65
missed 74
missile 100

mist 74
mistake 66
mistletoe 100
mistook 21
mite 68
mix 74
moan 14
moat 20
mob 61
mobile 100
mock 65
mocks 41
mode 94
mole 50
molecule 86
Monday 124
money 52
money 112
monk 113
monkey 112
monkeys 42
monologue 29
monstrous 115
moo 128
mood 40
mooed 40
moon 75
mop 99
mope 96
moped 91
more 98
morn 22
mosquito 100
moss 16
most 86
motel 120
mother 17
motorway 124

mould 82
mound 96
mountaineer 32
mouse 54
mow 100
mowed 94
mows 80
muck 30
mud 75
muffin 122
mug 61
mule 86
multiply 110
mum 75
mumble 96
munch 70
muse 116
mush 97
mushroom 95
musketeer 32
must 30
mute 15
my 110
myself 33
mysterious 115
mystify 110

N
nab 23
nag 39
nail 106
name 76
nan 117
nap 71
near 32
nearby 110
neat 72
neck 78
need 120

neigh 124
neighbour-hood 54
neighed 101
nephew 128
Neptune 75
nerd 12
nervous 115
nest 118
net 60
nettle 78
never 33
new 128
news 116
newt 15
nice 56
nicks 74
night 68
nightingale 106
nightmare 8
nil 58
nincompoop 54
nine 79
nip 128
nit 49
no 100
nomad 27
none 105
nook 21
noon 75
nor 98
norm 104
nose 80
not 87
note 20
nought 103
noun 112
now 23
nude 40
numb 75
nun 105

nursed 39
nut 55
nutmeg 67

O
oak 81
oar 98
oat 20
obey 124
obeyed 101
oblong 101
oboe 100
oboes 80
obsessed 118
obtain 90
obvious 115
occur 44
octopus 115
ode 94
offend 33
office 65
oil 81
oil rig 12
OK 124
old 82
omelette 60
omit 49
one 105
onslaught 103
ooze 116
operate 45
oppress 30
or 98
orang-utan 117
orbit 49
ordeal 122
ore 98
organise 123
origin 122
ornament 108

ostrich 59
other 17
otter 44
ought 103
ounce 16
our 111
out 83
outdoor 98
outfit 49
outlaw 98
outrage 84
outright 68
overhang 10
overlap 71
ow! 23
owe 100
owed 94
owl 83
own 14
ox 41
ozone 14

P
pa 18
pace 34
paced 85
pack 13
packed 8
pact 8
pad 27
page 84
paid 101
pail 106
pain 90
paint 85
pair 8
pale 106
pall 119
palm 10
Pam 60
pan 117
pancake 66
pane 90

pang 10
pant 10
pantomime 111
paperclip 128
parachute 15
parade 101
paradise 56
parakeet 72
parallel 120
park 28
part 19
pass 46
passed 66
passport 103
past 66
paste 85
pat 49
patch 19
paté 124
patio 100
patrolled 82
Paul 119
pave 20
paw 98
pawn 22
pay 124
pea 112
peach 11
peak 102
peal 122
pear 8
pearl 46
peas 42
peat 72
peck 78
pedigree 112
peek 102
peel 122
peep 63
peer 32

peg 67
pelt 12
pen 49
penguin 122
perform 104
perfume 95
perish 39
permit 49
persevere 32
persuade 101
pert 99
Peru 129
pest 118
pet 60
petal 78
petrifies 123
petrify 110
pew 128
phew 128
Phil 58
phoenix 74
phone 14
photo 100
piano 100
pick 89
pickle 109
picks 74
pickup 114
pie 110
pier 32
pies 123
pig 12
piggyback 13
pigsty 110
pike 12
pile 100
pill 58
pillow 100
pin 122
pine 79
pined 36

ping 64
pink 59
pioneer 32
pip 128
pit 49
pit-a-pat 49
pitch 59
pixie 112
place 34
placed 85
plain 90
plan 117
plane 90
plank 11
planned 48
plaque 13
plate 45
platoon 75
played 101
playful 88
playwright 68
plea 112
plead 120
please 42
pleat 72
plight 68
plop 99
plot 87
plough 23
ploy 112
pluck 30
plug 61
plum 75
plumb 75
plume 95
plump 61
plunder 114
plus 115
plush 97
pocket 60
poke 81
pole 50

polite 68
poll 50
polled 82
pollute 15
pond 85
pong 101
pool 86
pop 99
pope 96
pore 98
pork 107
porridge 16
port 103
pose 80
possess 30
possessed 118
post 86
postcard 126
postpone 14
pot 87
potato 100
potatoes 80
pounce 16
pound 96
pour 98
poured 69
pout 83
pow 23
power 111
pox 41
practice 65
pram 60
prance 27
prank 11
pray 124
prayed 101
prayer 8
preach 11
precious 115
precise 56
preen 89
prefer 44

preferred 12
prepare 8
present 108
press 30
pressed 118
pretend 33
prevent 108
prey 124
preyed 101
price 56
prick 89
prickle 109
pricks 74
pride 92
prim 105
prime 111
primp 59
princess 30
print 87
prise 123
prize 123
proceed 120
profile 100
profound 96
program 60
progress 30
progressed 118
promise 65
promote 20
prone 14
prong 101
pronounce 16
prop 99
propel 120
propose 80
prose 80
protest 118
provide 92
provoke 81
prowl 83
prune 75

pry 110
pseudonym 105
pub 47
puff 88
puffin 122
pull 88
pump 61
pumpkin 122
pun 105
punch 70
punish 39
punk 113
punt 55
pup 114
puppet 60
purr 44
purred 12
pursued 40
pus 115
putt 55
pyramid 67
pyre 38

Q

quack 13
quacked 8
quadruped 91
quagmire 38
quail 106
quaint 85
quake 66
quart 103
quay 112
queen 89
quell 120
quest 118
queue 128
queues 116
quick 89
quid 67

quill 58
quip 128
quit 49
quite 68
quiver 93
quote 20

R

rabbit 49
raccoon 75
race 34
raced 85
rack 13
radio 100
radios 80
radius 115
rag 39
rage 84
raid 101
rail 106
railway 124
rain 90
rainbow 100
rake 66
ram 60
ramp 104
rampage 84
ran 117
rang 10
rank 11
rant 10
rap 71
rapid 67
rare 8
rash 24
rat 49
rat-a-tat-tat 49
rate 45
raucous 115
rave 20
ravenous 115

raw 98
ray 124
reach 11
react 8
read 91
read 120
real 122
realize 123
reap 63
rear 32
rebel 120
reboot 15
recent 108
recipe 112
recite 68
recline 79
recognize 123
recoil 81
recommend 33
record 69
red 91
redeem 29
reed 120
reek 102
reel 122
referee 112
refereed 120
referees 42
refrain 90
refugee 112
refuse 116
regard 126
regret 60
rehearsed 39
reign 90
rein 90
released 33
relent 108
rely 110
remain 90
remark 28

remind 36
remote 20
rendezvous 129
renowned 96
rent 108
repair 8
repeat 72
replace 34
replaced 85
replies 123
reply 110
report 103
reptile 100
request 118
rescued 40
resent 108
resign 79
resist 74
resort 103
respond 85
rest 118
restaurant 10
retreat 72
return 115
reveal 122
revere 32
revise 123
revive 39
revue 128
reward 69
rewind 36
rhyme 111
rice 56
rich 59
ricochet 124
rid 67
riddle 73
ride 92
ridge 16
ridicule 86
rig 12

right 68
rigid 67
rim 105
rind 36
ring 64
rink 59
rip 128
rise 123
river 93
road 94
roar 98
roared 69
roast 86
rob 61
robin 122
robot 87
rock 65
rocket 60
rocks 41
rode 94
rodeo 100
role 50
roll 50
rolled 82
rook 21
room 95
root 15
rope 96
rose 80
rot 87
rote 20
rough 88
round 96
rout 83
routine 89
row 23
row 100
rowed 94
rows 80
Roy 112
royal 81
rub 47
rubbish 39

rubble 17
rucksack 13
rude 40
rue 128
rug 61
ruin 122
rule 86
rum 75
rumble 96
rump 61
run 105
rung 70
runny 52
runt 55
ruse 116
rush 97
rust 30
rut 55

S
sachet 124
sack 13
sacked 8
sacrifice 56
sad 27
sag 39
sage 84
said 91
sail 106
saint 85
sake 66
saloon 75
salute 15
Sam 60
same 76
sand 48
sane 90
sang 10
sank 11
sap 71
sardine 89
sarong 101
sash 24

sat 49
satin 122
satisfy 110
save 20
saw 98
sawn 22
say 124
scab 23
scaffold 82
scale 106
scam 60
scamp 104
scan 117
scanned 48
scant 10
scar 18
scare 8
scarecrow 100
scarred 126
scary 48
scene 89
scent 108
schedule 86
scheme 29
school 86
scold 82
scoop 54
scoot 15
scope 96
score 98
scoreboard 69
scored 69
scorn 22
Scot 87
scour 111
scout 83
scowl 83
scram 60
scrap 71
scrape 46
scratch 19

scrawl 119
scream 29
screech 11
screen 89
screw 128
screwed 40
screws 116
scrimp 59
scroll 50
scrub 47
scruff 88
scrum 75
scrunch 70
scud 75
scuff 88
scum 75
sea 112
seal 122
seam 29
seas 42
seat 72
secret 60
see 112
seed 120
seek 102
seem 29
seen 89
seep 63
sees 42
seesaw 98
seize 42
self 33
selfish 39
sell 120
send 33
sent 108
separate 45
sequin 122
serene 89
serious 115
service 65
serviette 60
set 60

settee *112*
settle *78*
sever *33*
severe *32*
sew *100*
sewn *14*
sews *80*
shack *13*
shade *101*
shadow *100*
shadows *80*
shake *66*
shallow *100*
sham *60*
shame *76*
shampoo *128*
shampooed *40*
shape *46*
shard *126*
share *8*
shark *28*
shave *20*
shawl *119*
she *112*
shear *32*
shed *91*
sheen *89*
sheep *63*
sheer *32*
sheet *72*
shelf *33*
shell *120*
shin *122*
shine *79*
ship *128*
shirt *99*
shiver *93*
shoal *50*
shock *65*
shocks *41*

shockwave *20*
shoe *129*
shoelace *34*
shoo *128*
shooed *40*
shook *21*
shoot *15*
shootout *83*
shop *99*
shore *98*
shorn *22*
short *103*
shot *87*
should *54*
shout *83*
shove *70*
show *100*
showed *94*
shower *111*
shown *14*
shows *80*
shrank *11*
shred *91*
shrew *128*
shriek *102*
shrill *58*
shrimp *59*
shrine *79*
shrink *59*
shrub *47*
shrug *61*
shrunk *113*
shun *105*
shunt *55*
shush *97*
shut *55*
shy *110*
sick *89*
sickle *109*
side *92*
sigh *110*
sighed *92*

sighs *123*
sight *68*
sign *79*
signed *36*
signpost *86*
sill *58*
sin *122*
sincere *32*
sinew *128*
sing *64*
sink *59*
sinner *29*
sip *128*
sir *44*
sit *49*
site *68*
six *74*
size *123*
skate *45*
skateboard *69*
skew *128*
ski *112*
skid *67*
skies *123*
skill *58*
skim *105*
skimp *59*
skin *122*
skint *87*
skip *128*
skirt *99*
skis *42*
skunk *113*
sky *110*
slab *23*
slack *13*
slam *60*
slang *10*
slap *71*
slapdash *24*
slash *24*
slate *45*

slave *20*
sled *91*
sleek *102*
sleep *63*
sleet *72*
sleigh *124*
slept *26*
slew *128*
slewed *40*
slice *56*
slick *89*
slid *67*
slide *92*
slight *68*
slim *105*
slime *111*
sling *64*
slink *59*
slip *128*
slipper *44*
sliver *93*
slog *29*
sloop *54*
slop *99*
slope *96*
slot *87*
slow *100*
slowed *94*
slows *80*
slug *61*
slum *75*
slump *61*
slung *70*
slunk *113*
slur *44*
slush *97*
sly *110*
smack *13*
smacked *8*
small *119*
smart *19*
smash *24*
smear *32*

smell *120*
smile *100*
smoke *81*
smother *17*
smug *61*
snack *13*
snacked *8*
snag *39*
snail *106*
snake *66*
snap *71*
snare *8*
snatch *19*
sneak *102*
sneer *32*
sneeze *42*
snip *128*
snitch *59*
snob *61*
snoop *54*
snooze *116*
snore *98*
snored *69*
snort *103*
snot *87*
snout *83*
snow *100*
snowed *94*
snowflake *66*
snows *80*
snub *47*
snuff *88*
snug *61*
so *100*
soak *81*
soap *96*
soar *98*
soared *69*
sob *61*
sock *65*
socks *41*
software *8*
soil *81*

sold *82*
sole *50*
soled *82*
solitaire *8*
solitude *40*
solo *100*
some *75*
someone *105*
son *105*
song *101*
soon *75*
sore *98*
sorrow *100*
sort *103*
sought *103*
soul *50*
sound *96*
soundtrack *13*
soup *54*
sour *111*
souvenir *32*
sow *23*
sow *100*
sown *14*
sows *80*
space *34*
spaced *85*
spade *101*
Spain *90*
span *117*
spank *11*
spanned *48*
spar *18*
spare *8*
spark *28*
sparred *126*
spat *49*
speak *102*
spear *32*
speck *78*
sped *91*
speech *11*

speed *120*
spell *120*
spelt *12*
spend *33*
spent *108*
spice *56*
spied *92*
spies *123*
spike *12*
spill *58*
spin *122*
spine *79*
spinner *29*
spire *38*
spit *49*
spite *68*
splash *24*
splat *49*
spleen *89*
splice *56*
splint *87*
split *49*
spoil *81*
spoke *81*
spool *86*
spoon *75*
sport *103*
spouse *54*
spout *83*
sprain *90*
sprang *10*
sprawl *119*
spray *124*
sprayed *101*
spread *91*
spree *112*
sprig *12*
spring *64*
sprint *87*
sprite *68*
sprout *83*
sprung *70*
spud *75*

spun *105*
spur *44*
spurn *115*
spurt *99*
spy *110*
squall *119*
square *8*
squat *87*
squawk *107*
squeak *102*
squeal *122*
squeeze *42*
squid *67*
squint *87*
squire *38*
squirt *99*
squish *39*
stab *23*
stable *106*
stack *13*
stacked *8*
stag *39*
stage *84*
stagefright *68*
staid *101*
stain *90*
stair *8*
staircase *34*
stake *66*
stale *106*
stalk *107*
stall *119*
stamp *104*
stampede *120*
Stan *117*
stance *27*
stand *48*
stank *11*
star *18*
stare *8*
starred *126*

start *19*
state *45*
statue *128*
stay *124*
stayed *101*
steak *66*
steal *122*
steam *29*
steed *120*
steel *122*
steep *63*
steer *32*
stepped *26*
stereo *100*
stereos *80*
stern *115*
stew *128*
stews *116*
stick *89*
sticks *74*
stile *100*
still *58*
sting *64*
stink *59*
stir *44*
stirred *12*
stitch *59*
stoat *20*
stock *65*
stocks *41*
stole *50*
stone *14*
stood *54*
stool *86*
stoop *54*
stop *99*
store *98*
stored *69*
stork *107*
storm *104*
stout *83*
stow *100*

stowaway *124*
stowed *94*
stows *80*
straight *45*
straightaway *124*
strain *90*
strand *48*
strap *71*
straw *98*
strayed *101*
streak *102*
stream *29*
street *72*
stress *30*
stressed *118*
strewn *75*
stride *92*
strike *12*
string *64*
strip *128*
strive *39*
strode *94*
stroke *81*
stroll *50*
strolled *82*
strong *101*
struck *30*
strum *75*
strung *70*
strut *55*
stub *47*
stubble *17*
stuck *30*
stud *75*
studio *100*
stuff *88*
stumble *96*
stump *61*
stun *105*
stung *70*
stunk *113*

stunt *55*
stupid *67*
sty *110*
style *100*
subdue *128*
substitute *15*
subtract *8*
subway *124*
succeed *120*
success *30*
succumb *75*
suck *30*
sud *75*
sue *128*
sued *40*
suede *101*
suggest *118*
suit *15*
suitcase *34*
sum *75*
summit *49*
sun *105*
Sunday *124*
sung *70*
sunk *113*
sunny *52*
sunrise *123*
sup *114*
supply *110*
support *103*
suppose *80*
supreme *29*
surprise *123*
surround *96*
survey *124*
surveyed *101*
survive *39*
suspend *33*
swag *39*
swam *60*
swap *99*
swarm *104*

swat *87*
sway *124*
swear *8*
sweat *60*
swede *120*
sweep *63*
sweet *72*
swell *120*
swept *26*
swig *12*
swill *58*
swim *105*
swine *79*
swing *64*
swirl *46*
swish *39*
switch *59*
swoon *75*
swoop *54*
sword *69*
swore *98*
sworn *22*
swot *87*
swum *75*
swung *70*
synonym *105*

T
table *106*
tack *13*
tact *8*
tadpole *50*
tag *39*
tai-kwando *129*
tail *106*
taint *85*
take *66*
takeaway *124*
tale *106*
talk *107*

158

tall *119*
tame *76*
tan *117*
tang *10*
tangerine *89*
tank *11*
tanned *48*
tap *71*
tape *46*
tar *18*
tarmac *13*
tarred *126*
tart *19*
task *10*
taste *85*
tattoo *128*
tattooed *40*
tattoos *116*
taught *103*
taut *103*
tea *112*
teach *11*
team *29*
tear *32*
teas *42*
tease *42*
technique *102*
Ted *91*
tee *112*
teem *29*
teen *89*
teenage *84*
telescope *96*
tell *120*
telltale *106*
ten *49*
tend *33*
tent *108*
terrified *92*
terrifies *123*
terrify *110*
Terry *73*

test *118*
than *117*
thank *11*
that *49*
thatch *19*
thaw *98*
their *8*
theme *29*
then *49*
there *8*
therefore *98*
these *42*
they *124*
thick *89*
thigh *110*
thighs *123*
thin *122*
thing *64*
think *59*
thinner *29*
third *12*
thirst *39*
thirteen *89*
this *65*
thorn *22*
those *80*
though *100*
thought *103*
thrash *24*
thread *91*
threat *60*
three *112*
threw *128*
thrill *58*
throat *20*
throb *61*
throne *14*
throng *101*
through *129*
throughout *83*
throw *100*
thrown *14*

throws *80*
thrush *97*
thrust *30*
thud *75*
thug *61*
thumb *75*
thump *61*
thunder *114*
thus *115*
thwart *103*
thyme *111*
tick *89*
ticket *60*
tickle *109*
ticks *74*
tick-tock *65*
tide *92*
tie *110*
tied *92*
ties *123*
tiger *44*
tight *68*
tightrope *96*
tile *100*
till *58*
Tim *105*
time *111*
timetable *106*
timezone *14*
timid *67*
tin *122*
tint *87*
tiptoes *80*
tire *38*
tissue *128*
toad *94*
toadstool *86*
toast *86*
today *124*
toe *100*
toes *80*
toffee *112*

toffees *42*
toil *81*
told *82*
tomahawk *107*
tomb *95*
tombstone *14*
tomorrow *100*
ton *105*
tone *14*
tong *101*
tongue *70*
tonight *68*
too *128*
took *21*
tool *86*
toot *15*
toothache *66*
top *99*
tore *98*
torment *108*
torn *22*
tornado *100*
toss *16*
tot *87*
tough *88*
tourist *74*
tow *100*
toward *69*
towed *94*
towel *83*
tower *111*
town *112*
tows *80*
toy *112*
trace *34*
traced *85*
track *13*
tracked *8*
trade *101*
trail *106*

train *90*
tram *60*
tramp *104*
trampoline *89*
trance *27*
tranquil *58*
transport *103*
trap *71*
trapeze *42*
trash *24*
trawl *119*
tray *124*
tread *91*
treat *72*
tree *112*
trees *42*
trek *78*
tremendous *115*
trend *33*
trespass *46*
tress *30*
trial *100*
trice *56*
trick *89*
trickle *109*
tricks *74*
tried *92*
tries *123*
trike *12*
trim *105*
trip *128*
troll *50*
trombone *14*
troop *54*
trot *87*
trouble *17*
trounce *16*
trout *83*
trowel *83*
truck *30*

true *128*
trump *61*
trumpet *60*
trunk *113*
trust *30*
try *110*
tsar *18*
tub *47*
tuck *30*
tug *61*
tulip *128*
tum *75*
tumble *96*
tune *75*
turmoil *81*
turn *115*
tut-tut *55*
tutu *129*
twang *10*
tweed *120*
twice *56*
twiddle *73*
twig *12*
twilight *68*
twin *122*
twine *79*
twirl *46*
twist *74*
twit *49*
twitch *59*
tycoon *75*
typhoon *75*
tyre *38*

U
UFO *100*
UFOs *80*
umpire *38*
under *114*
understand *48*
understood *54*

undid 67
unfair 8
unfurled 46
unicorn 22
uniform 104
unique 102
unite 68
unkind 36
unless 30
unpack 13
unpacked 8
untie 110
until 58
unwell 120
unwrap 71
up 114
upright 68
upset 60
upstage 84
uptight 68
urn 115
us 115
use 116
useful 88
utmost 86

V
vain 90
valentine 79
valley 112
value 128
vampire 38
van 117
vane 90
vanish 39
various 115
vary 48
vast 66
vat 49
veal 122
veer 32
veil 106
vein 90

vent 108
venue 128
very 73
vest 118
vet 60
vice 56
video 100
videos 80
view 128
viewed 40
views 116
vile 100
vine 79
violin 122
virus 115
visit 49
vitamin 122
volcano 100
volcanoes 80
vole 50
volunteer 32
voodoo 128
vote 20
vow 23
vowel 83

W
wade 101
wag 39
wage 84
wail 106
waist 85
wait 45
wake 66
walk 107
wall 119
walrus 115
wand 85
war 98
ward 69
warm 104
wart 103
wary 48

waste 85
wave 20
way 124
we 112
weak 102
wean 89
wear 8
website 68
wed 91
wee 112
weed 120
week 102
weep 63
weigh 124
weighed 101
weight 45
weir 32
well 120
welt 12
went 108
wept 26
were 44
west 118
wet 60
whack 13
whacked 8
whale 106
wham 60
what 87
whatever 33
wheat 72
wheel 122
wheeze 42
when 49
whenever 33
where 8
wherever 33
which 59
whichever 33
while 100
whim 105
whine 79
whined 36

whip 128
whiplash 24
whirl 46
whirligig 12
whirlpool 86
whirr 44
whirred 12
white 68
whoever 33
whole 50
whom 95
whoop 54
whose 116
why 110
wick 89
wide 92
widespread 91
wig 12
wigwam 60
will 58
wimp 59
win 122
wind 36
windmill 58
window 100
wine 79
wing 64
wink 59
winner 29
wire 38
wise 123
wish 39
wit 49
witch 59
within 122
without 83
woe 100
woes 80
woke 81
womb 95
wombat 49
won 105

wonder 114
wonderful 88
wondrous 115
woo 128
wood 54
wooed 40
wool 88
word 12
wore 98
worn 22
worst 39
would 54
wound 96
wow 23
wrap 71
wreck 78
wren 49
wring 64
wrist 74
write 68
wrong 101
wrote 20
wrung 70
wry 110

X
X-ray 124
X-rayed 101
xylophone 14

Y
yacht 87
yak 13
yam 60
yank 11
yap 71
yard 126
yawn 22
yearn 115
yeast 33

yell 120
yellow 127
yen 49
yes 30
yesterday 124
yet 60
yoke 81
yolk 81
yoo-hoo 128
young 70
your 98
yourself 33
yowl 83
yo-yo 100
yuck 30
yule 86
yum 75
yum-yum 75

Z
zap 71
zeal 122
zero 100
zest 118
zigzag 39
zinc 59
zing 64
zip 128
zone 14
zoo 128-9
zoom 95
zoos 116